Using Research for Strategic Planning

Norman P. Uhl, *Editor*

NEW DIRECTIONS FOR INSTITUTIONAL RESEARCH
Sponsored by the Association for Institutional Research
MARVIN W. PETERSON, *Editor-in-Chief*

Number 37, March 1983

Paperback sourcebooks in
The Jossey-Bass Higher Education Series

Jossey-Bass Inc., Publishers
San Francisco • Washington • London

Norman P. Uhl (Ed.).
Using Research for Strategic Planning.
New Directions for Institutional Research, no. 37.
San Francisco: Jossey-Bass, 1983

New Directions for Institutional Research Series
Marvin W. Peterson, *Editor-in-Chief*

New Directions for Institutional Research (publication number
USPS 098-830) is published quarterly by Jossey-Bass Inc.,
Publishers, and is sponsored by the Association for Institutional
Research. The volume and issue numbers above are included for
the convenience of libraries. Second-class postage rates paid at
San Francisco, California, and at additional mailing offices.

Correspondence:
Subscriptions, single-issue orders, change of address notices,
undelivered copies, and other correspondence should be sent to
New Directions Subscriptions, Jossey-Bass Inc., Publishers,
433 California Street, San Francisco, California 94104.

Editorial correspondence should be sent to the Editor-in-Chief,
Marvin W. Peterson, Center for the Study of Higher Education,
University of Michigan, Ann Arbor, Michigan 48109.

Library of Congress Catalogue Card Number LC 82-84191
International Standard Serial Number ISSN 0271-0579
International Standard Book Number ISBN 87589-955-2

Cover art by Willi Baum
Manufactured in the United States of America

Ordering Information

The paperback sourcebooks listed below are published quarterly and can be ordered either by subscription or as single copies.

Subscriptions cost $35.00 per year for institutions, agencies, and libraries. Individuals can subscribe at the special rate of $21.00 per year *if payment is by personal check.* (Note that the full rate of $35.00 applies if payment is by institutional check, even if the subscription is designated for an individual.) Standing orders are accepted.

Single copies are available at $7.95 when payment accompanies order, and *all single-copy orders under $25.00 must include payment.* (California, Washington, D.C., New Jersey, and New York residents please include appropriate sales tax.) For billed orders, cost per copy is $7.95 plus postage and handling. (Prices subject to change without notice.)

To ensure correct and prompt delivery, all orders must give either the *name of an individual* or an *official purchase order number.* Please submit your order as follows:

Subscriptions: specify series and subscription year.
Single Copies: specify sourcebook code and issue number (such as, IR8).

Mail orders for United States and Possessions, Latin America, Canada, Japan, Australia, and New Zealand to:
> Jossey-Bass Inc., Publishers
> 433 California Street
> San Francisco, California 94104

Mail orders for all other parts of the world to:
> Jossey-Bass Limited
> 28 Banner Street
> London EC1Y 8QE

New Directions for Institutional Research Series
Marvin W. Peterson, *Editor-in-Chief*

IR1 *Evaluating Institutions for Accountability,* Howard R. Bowen
IR2 *Assessing Faculty Effort,* James I. Doi
IR3 *Toward Affirmative Action,* Lucy W. Sells
IR4 *Organizing Nontraditional Study,* Samuel Baskin
IR5 *Evaluating Statewide Boards,* Robert O. Berdahl
IR6 *Assuring Academic Progress Without Growth,* Allan M. Cartter
IR7 *Responding to Changing Human Resource Needs,* Paul Heist, Jonathan R. Warren
IR8 *Measuring and Increasing Academic Productivity,* Robert A. Wallhaus
IR9 *Assessing Computer-Based System Models,* Thomas R. Mason
IR10 *Examining Departmental Management,* James Smart, James Montgomery
IR11 *Allocating Resources Among Departments,* Paul L. Dressel, Lou Anna Kimsey Simon
IR12 *Benefiting from Interinstitutional Research,* Marvin W. Peterson

Contents

Two questions — "What does strategic planning involve, and what is the role of the institutional researcher?"— are addressed, and a preview of the following chapters is presented.

Editor's Introduction: Institutional Research and Strategic Planning

Norman P. Uhl

Effective strategic planning depends on information. Misunderstandings about the relationship between institutional research and institutional planning usually cause only limited information to be available at the different stages of planning and decision making. Too often, institutional researchers provide pages of data, but not the necessary information. As a result, those responsible for planning are frequently unaware of the information that can be made available. This sourcebook attempts to show institutional researchers, as well as others involved in any part of the planning process, the valuable contributions that institutional research can make to planning.

Identifying the Process of Strategic Planning

While Fincher (1982) indicates that there are several different definitions of strategic planning in the planning literature, the authors of this sourcebook consider strategic planning, long-range planning, and master planning as synonymous. Steiner (1979), a leading authority on planning, supports this approach, as do Peterson (1980), Green and others (1979), Lindberg (1979), and Cope (1978). Strategic planning can be described as an

N. P. Uhl (Ed.). *Using Research for Strategic Planning.* New Directions for
Institutional Research, no. 37. San Francisco: Jossey-Bass, March 1983.

analytical approach that encompasses an assessment of the future (usually five to ten years ahead), the determination of desired goals in the context of the future, the development of alternative courses of action to achieve those goals, and the selection of courses of action from among those alternatives. It is a continuous process that includes feedback and evaluation of the degree to which the goals are being achieved. Strategic planning has two major purposes: to obtain agreement on specific long-range institutional goals and to provide advice to the president and the board of trustees concerning activities that should be given priority in annual budgets. While strategic planning is useless if it does not influence the budget, it is also important to realize that planning and budgeting are two separate processes.

Strategic planning can be performed at different levels of formality and with differing degrees of faculty involvement. What may be an excellent planning procedure for one institution may be totally ineffective for another. Regardless of the specific procedures employed, however, there are four major phases that should be included in any planning system: (1) the analysis phase, which includes the assessment of the external and internal environments, (2) the mission-and-goals phase, (3) the objectives and action-plans phase, and (4) the resource-use, needs-analysis, and expenditure-strategies phase.

The analysis phase includes an assessment of the institution's past and present situations and of its projected future. It involves an analysis of the internal and external environments. Assessment of the external environment involves identifying the external threats and opportunities that face not only the institution as a whole, but also its component parts. These external factors may include economic, social, technological, political, legal, demographic, and competitive forces. Assessment of the internal environment may vary from institution to institution, because schools can differ widely in their programs and internal operations. Some areas to be assessed are projections of student enrollments and revenues, the values and styles of the administration, student and faculty values and characteristics, the strengths and weaknesses of the institution and of individual departments and units, performance of special studies of institutional operations, and evaluation of planning strategies (for example, attempting to improve student retention). Analysis of physical facilities is also part of this phase. As Shirley and Volkwein (1978) indicate, matching the internal strengths and weaknesses (what an institution *can* do) to the external environmental opportunities and constraints (what an instituion *could* do) and to its constituents' personal values (what an institution *wants* to do) results in strategic decisions.

The mission-and-goals phase includes the development of a mission statement and associated broad-based goals. The mission statement, in as specific a form as is practical, provides the purposes of the organization. While broad in scope and covering a long period of time, the statement is not unchangeable and should be re-examined and updated, as necessary. The results of the analysis phase are useful for re-examining a mission statement. From the mission statement, a set of broad goals is derived, which identifies a desired state or future condition and which normally covers a two- to five-year period. This set of goals indicates the institution's intention of taking suitable action to narrow the gap between what the institution is and what it should be. These goals often can be stated in terms of performance. Thus, they can be documented quantitatively. Even qualitative goals can be assessed. Whatever goals are developed, they should be re-examined periodically to determine whether or not they are being achieved.

The third phase is the objectives and action-plans phase. Objectives relate to goals and are the means by which the goals are achieved. An objective is an operational indicator of a goal that is quantitatively defined. Objectives are usually for a one-year period and are developed to achieve goals, such as directing the growth of an activity or reaching certain levels of performance. Action plans are generated from these objectives; when accomplished, they should contribute to the achievement of objectives. These action plans fix responsibility for specific actions and thereby build accountability into this phase of the planning process.

The last phase is the resource-use, needs-analysis, and expenditure-strategies phase, which has two purposes — examining how resources are used in the institution's current operations and analyzing the need for resources used in the institution's strategic plan.

If all four phases of strategic planning were performed, there would be nine outcomes:

1. Information from the analysis of the external environment
2. Information from the analysis of the internal environment
3. Information from the facilities analysis
4. Recommended planning strategies
5. Updated mission statement
6. Statement of goals
7. Statement of objectives
8. Final revenue estimates
9. Expenditure priorities.

These four phases are explained well by Green and others (1979). A detailed description of how one institution completed these four phases is also presented by Uhl (1980).

Guide to the Following Chapters

Institutions may include these four planning phases with different degrees of formality and levels of participation. In most instances, the institutional researcher is not directly responsible for instititional planning, but it should be apparent from this brief overview of strategic planning that considerable information must be available for such planning to be successful. Institutional researchers cannot assume that all administrators will be equally aware of the important contributions that institutional research can make to planning. The best procedure for institutional researchers is to disseminate information that will assist the planning process. An examination of the four phases of planning will indicate some ways by which institutional research can provide significant input to the planning process.

The chapters in this sourcebook describe studies and/or methods that institutional research officers can use to make significant contributions to these phases of strategic planning.

The analysis phase is the area in which institutional research can have its greatest impact. Conducting numerous studies to analyze the external environment is beyond the capacity of most institutional research offices, but the information obtained from such studies is important for planning. Chapter Two discusses the importance of using results from studies performed by other agencies to assess variables considered relevant to planning and identifies external environmental variables found to be important, as well as some sources of information on these variables.

Unfortunately, it is not always possible to obtain all the necessary external data from other sources. In these cases, it may be necessary for an institutional research office to conduct its own study of part of the external environment. Chapter Three provides an example of the methodology for performing one such study, which is concerned with the possible marketing of a new academic program.

The assessment of the internal environment is also included in the analysis phase. The areas to be examined will vary from institution to institution, but usually include the strengths and weaknesses of academic departments, as well as of other organizational units; the reputation of an institution; projection of student enrollments; studies evaluating how well institutional goals are being achieved; the institutional climate; financial stability of the institution; the ability of decision makers to assess information; and the efficient use of personnel and facilities. In addition, certain analytical studies are necessary to evaluate present and proposed institutional policies. Examples of useful analytical studies may include the analysis of faculty salaries by department and rank; characteristics of new and old students (age, interests, career aspirations, and so forth); and patterns of enrollment by department.

Chapters Four, Five, and Six give examples of assessing different aspects of the internal environment. Chapter Four concentrates on academic program evaluation, Chapter Five explains facilities analysis, and Chapter Six gives several examples of assessing the degree to which institutional goals are achieved. Chapter Six is also concerned with part of the second and third phases — the development of institutional goals and action plans. It describes several ways of identifying goals, reaching agreement on goals that should receive highest priority, and discussing the development of action plans based on these goals.

All phases of strategic planning are very dependent on the quality of available information. Chapter Seven provides a method for communicating information to all decision makers, regardless of whether or not a computer-based management information system is available.

Chapter Eight describes how and when the Delphi technique can be used to assist in the different phases of planning. It is discussed as both a forecasting tool and a procedure for obtaining convergence of opinion.

Chapter Nine discusses implications for institutional research of developing a close working relationship with institutional planning. It also provides additional sources of the information that is already available to institutional researchers.

References

Cope, R. G. *Strategic Policy Planning.* Littleton, Colo.: Ireland Educational Corp., 1978.

Fincher, C. "What Is Strategic Planning?" *Research in Higher Education,* 1982, *16* (4), 373–376.

Green, J. L., Mayyar, D. P., and Ruch, R. S. *Strategic Planning and Budgeting for Higher Education.* La Jolla, Calif.: J. L. Green and Associates, 1979.

Lindberg, R. A. *Long-Range Planning.* New York: American Management Associations, 1979.

Peterson, M. W. "Analyzing Alternative Approaches to Planning." In P. Jedamus and M. W. Peterson (Eds.), *Improving Academic Management.* San Francisco: Jossey-Bass, 1980.

Shirley, R. C., and Volkwein, J. F. "Establishing Academic Program Priorities." *Journal of Higher Education,* 1978, *49* (5), 472–488.

Steiner, G. A. *Strategic Planning.* New York: Free Press, 1979.

Uhl, N. P. "Collecting and Applying Social and Economic Information." In L. L. Baird and R. T. Hartnett (Eds.), *Understanding Faculty and Student Life.* San Francisco: Jossey-Bass, 1980.

Norman P. Uhl is professor of education at Mount Saint Vincent University in Halifax, Nova Scotia. He was previously associate vice-chancellor for research, evaluation, and planning at North Carolina Central University and research psychologist with Educational Testing Service. He is coauthor of the Institutional Goals Inventory.

How does an institutional researcher assess the external environment?
One way is to take advantage of studies done by other agencies.
This chapter indicates available sources, gives an assessment classification
procedure, and provides sample excerpts of the results of such an assessment.

Assessing the External Environment

Robert H. Glover
Jeffrey Holmes

An important part of strategic or long-range planning is assessing the environment external to the institution. Planners do not have time to assess this external environment adequately, nor do institutional researchers have the time to conduct the numerous studies that would be necessary. Fortunately, statistics are already compiled, and many studies are performed by external agencies. The results can be used by institutional researchers to provide information for supporting an assessment of the external environment. It is the purpose of this chapter to identify some of these sources of information and to illustrate how the results of these studies can be presented to assist individuals charged with developing institutional plans.

State of the Art

The role of environment assessment in strategic planning is to identify environmental factors relevant to the mission of the institution; to assess favorable or unfavorable impacts of events, conditions, and trends on priorities; to develop scenarios; and to devise realistic strategies for creating viable futures for the institution.

N. P. Uhl (Ed.). *Using Research for Strategic Planning.* New Directions for
Institutional Research, no. 37. San Francisco: Jossey-Bass, March 1983.

While environmental assessment is widely recognized as a necessary step in strategic planning, in the literature more is said about environmental assessment and its use in strategic planning than about designing and implementing such an assessment. Utterbach (1979), in one of the few articles specifically about environmental assessment, notes more accent on quantitative forecasts of demographic, economic, and marketing variables than on qualitative forecasts of shifting values, lifestyles, and social and political change. He also emphasizes the tendency to focus on immediate decisions. An environmental assessment helps bring seemingly distant opportunities, constraints, and threats within the decision makers's frame of reference and planning horizon. In the same article, Utterbach reviews a variety of environmental assessment and forecasting techniques presented in the literature. These include quantifying expert opinion, extrapolating trends under varying constraints, formulating assumptions, monitoring the environment, and simulating the interaction of environmental variables and constraints.

Bell and Mau (1971) suggested a decision model that offers insights into the processes of perception, thinking, and learning involved in environmental assessment. Decision makers are influenced by their values; their orientations toward past, present, and future; their beliefs about cause and effect; their optimism or pessimism about possibilities for controlling events; their goals and expectations; and their reliance on intuition or on facts. Elegant models, however, cannot compensate for inadequate data gathering and interpretation. The validity of a forecast often depends on the diversity and quality of information sources. The need to integrate intuition and creative judgments with researched trends and data still makes environmental assessment more an art than a science (Utterbach, 1979).

Factors to Consider in Assessing the External Environment

Some important factors to be considered in assessing the external environment are the social context, institutional relationships, geographical scope, and time frame. These are briefly described below.

Social Context. The social context relevant to strategic planning includes opportunities, uncertainties, constraints, and threats that are significantly beyond the control of a single institution, but which demand an effective response. Because higher education is embedded in a social culture, a comprehensive structure is required to classify assumptions and trends. Categories suggested in recent environmental assessments and forecasts (American Association of State Colleges and Universities, 1978; Glover, 1979; Marien, 1976) are (1) demographic and geographic trends, (2) economic and financial factors, (3) natural resource and environmental protection, (4) politics and government, (5) international affairs and national defense, (6) law and justice, (7) values and lifestyles, (8) health and medicine, (9) science and technology,

(10) work and employment, (11) education and training, (12) equality of opportunity, and (13) culture, humanities, and the arts.

Institutional Relationships. Policy decisions on mission, goals, organization and policies, academic programs, and resource allocations are made internally, but, to varying degrees, institutions are influenced by or constrained in their relationships with their clienteles, resource suppliers, governing bodies, and competitors (Baldridge, 1971; Dill, 1958; Livingstone, 1970).

Geographical Scope. Depending on the mission, prestige, and visibility of the institution, geographical scope may be international, national, regional, or local—international and national for a sponsored-research university; regional and state for a public comprehensive university or a selective liberal arts college; and state and local for a private comprehensive university, a developing liberal arts college, or a public junior or community college.

Time Frame. The period selected for analysis may be short-range (three to five years), middle-range (five to ten years), or long-range (ten to twenty years). Obviously, the longer the period, the more difficult is is to achieve accuracy.

The Process of Assessment

Numerous techniques are available for gathering information to be used in an environmental assessment. These include open-ended interviews or questionnaires, literature searches and analyses, interdisciplinary panels, futures forums, futures surveys, and scenarios. Of these, literature searches and analyses are emphasized here, since this is the one technique that will allow an institutional researcher to assess the overall external environment within a reasonable period of time. Occasionally, specific studies of the external environment are required; some techniques that may be used for such studies are discussed in Chapters Three and Eight of this sourcebook.

Every assessment is biased by the values, beliefs, interests, and experiences of the institutional researcher and by those of each administrator who interprets assumptions and trends. The institutional researcher should make certain that credible and balanced sources are used. For critical decisions in a complex and uncertain environment, it is sometimes helpful to include both optimistic and pessimistic scenarios. A comprehensive example of such scenarios is provided later in this chapter.

A strategy or a specific mode of operation is required for an efficient literature search. Moreover, forecasts and trends data are widely scattered. Fortunately, there are computer-search services, indexes, bibliographies, and policy research centers that concentrate such information and enable researchers to develop the necessary strategies.

In a computer search of Educational Resource Information Center (ERIC) and Current Index to Journals in Education (CIJE) abstracts, several key phrases—"futures (of society)," "trend analysis," and "social indicators"— yield a high return of policy research and forecast information. Adding the key phrase "higher education" in combination with an organizational descriptor such as "state coordinating board," "liberal arts college," or "state universities" will select applications to specific institutional environments. Content can be restricted still more by the use of such key phrases as "enrollment trends," "college students," "college faculty," "employment," "educational finance," "curriculum development," and "resource allocation." ERIC microfiche and journal articles are readily and inexpensively retrieved.

The World Future Society has produced a guide to information sources, with separate indexes for organizations, individuals, and research projects (Cornish, 1977). A College Board handbook identifies educational research and policy research centers, as well as leading researchers (Willingham, 1973). Marien (1976) has prepared an annotated bibliography and critical guide to the literature on social directions. The World Future Society, with Marien as editor, also publishes the *Futures Survey,* a monthly abstract of books, articles, and reports.

For futures literature and trends data, the Library of Congress key phrases are "forecasting" and "social indicators." Additional key phrases can be incorporated — "population," "income," "employment," "economic," "public expenditures," and "college environment," for example. For contextual mapping of social trends, the *Yearbook of World Problems and Human Potential,* the yearbooks of the *Encyclopedia Americana,* the *Encyclopedia Britannica,* and the *New York Times Index* are useful. Federal, state, and local governments, as well as private profit-making corporations, university research and development centers, and private nonprofit higher education associations, are all in the forecasting business. The Joint Economic Committee of Congress has published a long-term forecast of economic growth (Joint Economic Committee on Development, 1978). Another source of this information is Hamrin (1980). A Sloan Foundation Commission on government and higher education has integrated environmental assessment with twenty-one institutional self-studies (Gruson, 1977, 1978, 1979; Spero, 1978). Centra (1978), a researcher at Educational Testing Service, has reviewed the enrollment forecasts of the National Center for Educational Statistics (NCES), the American Council on Education (ACE), the Carnegie Council, and of individual forecasters, including Bowen, Froomkin, and Dresch.

Data on student characteristics and educational and career aspirations are available through the National Center for Educational Statistics' National Longitudinal Study, the College Board and American College Testing Programs, and the American Council on Education UCLA American Freshman National Norms longitudinal studies.

The American Association for Higher Education (AAHE) and ERIC collaborate on a series covering current issues in higher education, and the *Chronicle of Higher Education* and *ACE Higher Education and National Affairs* also cover current issues and trends.

The National Center for Educational Statistics, the American Council on Education, and the Southern Regional Education Board all publish annual fact books.

Recent environmental assessments have been conducted by the College Board (Glover, 1979), the National Center for Research and Vocational Education (Lewis and Russell, 1981), the National Center for Higher Education Management Systems (Huckfeldt, 1972), the Institute for the Future (Johansen and Samuel, 1977), the Academy for Educational Development (Millett, 1978), and the Carnegie Foundation (1980).

Several organizations exist primarily to monitor futures forecasts and environmental trends—The World Future Society, the Futures Group, the Institute for the Future, Predicasts, Inc., the Congressional Clearing House on the Future, and the Institute of Life Insurance Trend Analysis Program. All maintain large data banks. The Futures Group and Predicasts, Inc., have data on line. Annual subscriptions and consulting fees for environmental assessment may be cost effective when one's own staff time and effort, as well as the benefits of high-quality assessment, are considered.

In Canada, the national agency Statistics Canada is a source of educational, demographic, and other societal data useful for forecasting. The Economic Council of Canada, the Institute for Research in Public Policy, the Association of Universities and Colleges of Canada, the Science Council of Canada, and various federal government departments produce reports that are also useful in this phase of the planning process. Further Canadian sources are included in the last chapter of this sourcebook.

Examples of Alternative Scenarios

The institutional researcher has to design an effective structure and process, locate information sources, help others gather data, consolidate information, and interpret the strategic implications. The following examples of scenarios may be useful as a guide to environmental considerations.

Optimistic Scenario (1990–2000). Americans will learn how to balance population growth with economic growth and resource scarcity. Through lifestyles which are more conserving of resources, they will also improve their standard of living.

Cooperation among government, business, and universities in space-age research and development will produce energy sources as alternatives to fossil fuels, with a reduction in energy dependence. Americans will drive less and use electronic communications more in business, education, and leisure.

Movement toward a technological, service-oriented society will increase the demand for people with advanced degrees. The oversupply in many professional fields will give way to shortages of manpower.

The birthrate trend will be reversed, and there will be a gradual increase in traditional college-age students seeking college admission. With a high percentage of the adult population already engaged in lifelong learning, colleges and universities will have to expand.

When technological breakthroughs are not forthcoming in areas of critical national need, massive basic research grants will go to major universities that have retained research capacity.

The selective liberal arts colleges with large endowments and the strictly denominational colleges will maintain their distinctive images and high academic standards, increasing their competitive advantages. Having acquired extensive experience in offering adult-learning opportunities, the faculties of liberal arts colleges will find ways to integrate younger, middle-aged, and older generations into a community of lifelong learners. A revitalized program of lifelong learning will become the mission of many liberal arts colleges, so as to meet the challenges presented by vocational education.

Flexible job arrangements, opportunities for job sharing, flexible work schedules, and reduced work weeks will provide more time for education and for family leisure activities. Midcareer job transitions, with periodic retraining, will become more common. Universities and employers will enable professionals to keep abreast of current trends or to train for new careers.

As the demand from full-time traditional students and part-time adult learners increases, competition between traditional and nontraditional education will give way to cooperation. Institutions will share facilities and resources to offer joint courses and to award credit for relevant formal or informal activities.

The focus in education will be on competence in locating and using information, thinking creatively and rationally, and communicating, rather than on retaining facts. A revitalization will occur in the liberal arts and in general education.

Pessimistic Scenario (1980–1990). The United States gross national product will increase at a slower rate than in the past two decades. Economic growth will be limited by a leveling in the productivity of workers, a decline in American technological superiority, and dependence on foreign nations for fuels and natural resources.

The pattern of recession combined with inflation will continue, with chronic unemployment and underemployment.

Declining birthrates will shift the population bulge from young (seventeen to twenty-five) to older (fifty-five and older) and cause intergenerational tension and conflict.

Affirmative action will be increasingly resisted both by employers and by the majority of employees as competition for jobs increases. A middle-class backlash will extend the taxpayers' revolt, limiting government growth.

Many public colleges will have to abandon open-door and low-tuition policies. Many private colleges will be forced to adopt open-door policies and to intensify the search for students who can afford high tuition.

Federal and state subsidies for private higher education will level off, in spite of lobbying by higher education consortia. Aid will not increase at a rate greater than inflation, and, with fewer students in the traditional college-age group, there will be reductions in funding.

Erosion of the economic value of a college degree, rising college costs, and the vocational orientation of youth will diminish the demand for admission to traditional colleges. Declining student enrollments will force liberal arts colleges to substitute job-related courses for traditional academic subjects.

Technological obsolescence and economic dislocation in industry will make it difficult to forecast future manpower needs. Students trained for specific vocations will find that their job skills quickly become obsolete, and they will need retraining.

Universities will have to cope with excess supply and underemployment in many professional fields. Competition for admission to high-status professions will be severe, as universities shift emphasis from graduate to undergraduate instruction and from research to teaching. Recent Ph.D. recipients and younger faculty members will be locked out of a tight academic job market.

Investment in research and development will increase at a rate slower than the rate of inflation. Proportionately more research funding will go to applied research in areas of high national need.

Many small private liberal arts colleges will not survive the 1980s. Some will go public or else will merge with other institutions.

Example of an External Environment Assessment

Student Enrollment. Individuals aged sixteen to twenty-four years will decline from 16.9 percent of the United States population (1977) to 14.8 percent (1985) to 12.1 percent (1990). This age group accounts for the majority of college students, work force volunteers, and heads of new households (Institute for the Future, 1979, pp. 4–5).

Student enrollment will be influenced by national and state politics, legal constraints, economic and employment trends, government regulation, state governance of higher education, institutional competition, and student consumer preferences (Spence, 1977).

Participation rates generally will increase more rapidly for women, adults, minorities, part-time students, foreign students, undergraduate degree programs, and nondegree programs (Carlson, 1980; Spence, 1977).

Faculty Supply and Demand. Reversal of the demand for teachers and the continued overall decline in job opportunities will create serious retrenchment problems for programs in the liberal arts and teacher education (Brooks, 1980).

Some experts believe service and information occupations are saturated (Joint Economic Committee on Development, 1978, pp. 4, 18, 19).

Public and academic interests conflict on institutional missions; the need for academic programs; duplication of programs and services; faculty salaries, tenure, and workloads; cost effectiveness; teaching, research, and public service priorities; employment of graduates; admissions and grading standards; and the impact of education on state goals for economic development (Gruson, 1979, p. 21).

Fund Raising. Of the $35 billion to $40 billion constituting the revenues of higher education institutions, $8 to $9 billion is made up of federal appropriations for financial aid to students. Hence, resource allocations to institutions are based more on student choice than on institutional preference (Deitch, 1978, pp. 109–110).

State appropriations for higher education have more than doubled in the last decade (from $7.5 to $19 billion), and gains consistently have exceeded inflation (Magarrell, 1980d, p. 7).

Alumni giving is highly concentrated in private institutions (and, recently, in some public universities and liberal arts colleges that enroll disproportionate numbers of high-income and high-ability students). Alumni giving is influenced by age and size of the institution, placement of graduates, loyalty engendered by the campus experience, established traditions of alumni giving, and organized fund-raising campaigns ("A Long View of Philanthropy," 1980, p. 4; Blau, 1973; Magarrell, 1980a, p. 1).

In 1979, gifts from individuals ($35.5 billion) far exceeded the philanthropic giving of profit-making corporations ($2.3 billion) and foundations ($2.2 billion). Endowment income is highly concentrated; about ninety private institutions have endowments over $5 million. The private sector obtains only a small amount of money from endowment earnings (Deitch, 1978; Magarrell, 1980c, p. 1).

Graduate/Career Placement. Underemployment of college-educated workers is likely to persist, as the surplus of young graduates will not be completely absorbed even by several years of recovery from recession (Joint Economic Committee on Development, 1978, pp. 5, 40–44).

Professional, managerial, and technical job opportunities have declined since 1971. Students of traditional college age (eighteen to twenty-four) may enroll in fewer numbers (Spence, 1977, p. 10).

Perceptions about graduates' jobs may be based on experiences gained at a time when only 25 percent of the population were graduates. As this ratio increases to 50 percent, college graduates will have to accept less desirable jobs (Deitch, 1978).

Government Regulation. Demands from federal and state agencies for information continue to proliferate. It is not clear that all the reports, reviews, and audits are productive (Gruson, 1979, p. 18).

Academic program reviews will provide a more rational basis for state priorities in higher education, considering budgetary constraints, employment opportunities for graduates, institutional missions and roles, student enrollment patterns, alternative funding sources, and resource allocation opportunities (Gruson, 1979, p. 56).

Emphasis on academic outcomes and costs will increase in response to executive, legislative, and student demands for disclosure of data on institutional effectiveness (Spence, 1977, p. 33).

Financial Expenditures. In 1980, the higher education price index increased by a record 9.9 percent, but the consumer price index increased at a still faster rate (Magarrell, 1980b, p. 14).

Faculty salaries, which account for 40 percent of general and educational expenses, have been increasing at a rate slower than inflation. Faculty salaries increased 202 percent between 1967 and 1979–1980 (Magarrell, 1980b, p. 14).

The major impacts of cost reduction efforts in higher education are deferred maintenance; failure to maintain faculty salaries at levels comparable to other professions; increased faculty workloads; use of reserve funds to meet current operating expenses; and reduced upkeep of buildings, grounds, and equipment (Magarrell, 1980b, p. 14).

Cooperation/Competition. Competition for students and funds will dominate the economics of higher education in the next decade (Deitch, 1978, p. 127).

Institutions that depend on tuition or enrollment and have excess capacity will experience financial threats to their survival (Deitch, 1978, p. 127).

Price competition with public institutions will place private institutions at a disadvantage unless the tuition gap is narrowed with federal and state student aid entitlements (Deitch, 1978, p. 127).

Academic Innovations. Integration of liberal education and career preparation is a task that all faculty members who teach undergraduates will have to confront. New models for general education and career preparation will be necessary as taxpayers, students, legislators, employers, and funding sources increasingly expect institutions to demonstrate that a college degree is worth its cost (Gaff, 1980, p. 2).

Curriculum development is especially complex during periods of economic retrenchment and declining student enrollment (Gaff, 1980, p. 2).

To reconstruct curricula, each institution has to design programs appropriate to its own circumstances and consistent with its own mission, traditions, character, needs, and faculty interests—under the constraints of employers, funding sources, and regulations (Gaff, 1980, p. 2).

Accreditation/Testing. Average scores on aptitude and achievement tests have declined in recent years, raising many issues about basic skills in the college-applicant pool, the quality of teaching in schools, and the impact of socio-cultural changes on learning (Wirtz, 1977).

A national commission recommended that, to revitalize accreditation, accrediting agencies state their purposes and criteria clearly; centralize coordination, monitoring, and supervision; make increasing use of independently appointed public representatives; conduct public hearings on policies and standards; and involve the professions in policy decisions and site visits (Miller, 1973).

Criticisms of regional and professional accrediting commissions include failure to distinguish between weak and strong institutions; negative evaluations that are rarely made public; the allegation that states are not receiving information necessary to decisions; and the perception that evaluators ignore public, administrative, and fiscal accountability (Magarrell, 1980b).

Collective Bargaining. Since 1967, about half the states have enacted legislation extending collective bargaining rights to faculty members in public higher education. Collective bargaining has been concentrated in six states where strong union traditions prevail—New York, Michigan, New Jersey, Washington, Illinois, and Wisconsin (Crossland, 1978).

Many forces are increasing faculty militancy and exerting pressure for collective bargaining. For example, faculty salaries lag behind inflation, professional autonomy and traditional prerogatives are being eroded, younger faculty members are locked out by the tenure system, declining enrollments are causing faculty layoffs, and faculty members are aware of union progress in raising teachers' salaries (Crossland, 1978).

The Role of the Institutional Researcher

The role of the institutional researcher as a facilitator of environmental assessment may be either centralized or decentralized. At one end of this continuum, the institutional researcher may design, implement, and report the results of an environmental assessment. This approach reduces the burden of planning on faculty members and administrators and ensures an institution-wide perspective. If administrators and faculty members are not involved in identifying the key strategic issues and variables, however, they may neither understand nor accept the environmental assessment.

As the size and complexity of institutions increases, the decentralized approach becomes more effective. Few institutional researchers have the knowledge or the time to produce balanced futures forecasts or to monitor important assumptions simultaneously for several schools or areas. The institutional researcher in the decentralized model has to provide leadership and coordination for environmental assessment. This effort involves designing an effective structure and process; locating information sources; and helping others gather data, consolidate information, and interpret the strategic implications.

References

"A Long View of Philanthropy." *Chronicle of Higher Education,* July 7, 1980, p. 4.

American Association of State Colleges and Universities. *A Futures-Creating Paradigm: A Guide to Long-Range Planning from the Future for the Future.* Washington, D.C.: American Association of State Colleges and Universities, Resource Center for Planned Change, 1978.

17

Baldridge, J. V. *Environmental Pressure, Professional Autonomy, and Coping Strategies in Academic Organizations.* Palo Alto, Calif.: Stanford University Center for Research and Development in Teaching, 1971.

Bell, W., and Mau, J. *The Sociology of the Future.* New York: Russell Sage Foundation, 1971.

Blau, P. M. *The Organization of Academic Work.* New York: Wiley, 1973.

Brooks, N. J. *The Future of Comprehensive Colleges and Universities.* Cambridge, Mass.: Sloan Commission on Government and Higher Education, 1980.

Carlson, D. E. *Student Access to Postsecondary Education: Comparative Analysis of Federal and State Student Aid Programs.* Washington, D.C.: Office of Planning and Budgeting, 1980.

Carnegie Foundation for the Advancement of Teaching. *Three Thousand Futures: The Next Twenty Years for Higher Education.* San Francisco: Jossey-Bass, 1980.

Centra, J. A. *College Enrollment in the 1980s: Projections and Possibilities.* Princeton, N.J.: College Entrance Examination Board, 1978.

Cornish, E. S. (Ed.). *The Future: A Guide to Information Sources.* Washington, D.C.: World Future Society, 1977.

Crossland, F. E. "Will the Academy Survive Unionization?" *Change Magazine,* 1978, *8* (1), 38-42.

Deitch, K. M. *Pricing and Financial Aid in Higher Education: Some Interactions.* Cambridge, Mass.: Sloan Commission on Government and Higher Education, 1978.

Dill, W. "Environment as an Influence on Managerial Autonomy." *Administrative Science Quarterly,* 1958, *2,* 409-443.

Gaff, J. G. (Ed.). *General Education Issues and Resources.* Washington, D.C.: Association of American Colleges, 1980.

Glover, R. H. *Alternative Scenarios of the American Future (1980-2000).* New York: The College Entrance Examination Board, 1979.

Gruson, E. S. *The National Politics of Higher Education.* Cambridge, Mass.: Sloan Commission on Government and Higher Education, 1977.

Gruson, E. S. *Developing Institutions: Background and Policy Alternatives.* Cambridge, Mass.: Sloan Commission on Government and Higher Education, 1978.

Gruson, E. S. *State Regulation of Higher Education in a Period of Decline.* Cambridge, Mass.: Sloan Commission on Government and Higher Education, 1979.

Hamrin, R. D. *Managing Growth in the 1980s: Toward a New Economics.* New York: Praeger, 1980.

Huckfeldt, V. E. *A Forecast of Changes in Postsecondary Education.* Boulder, Colo.: National Center for Higher Education Management Systems, 1972.

Institute for the Future. *Policy Choices in Vocational Education.* Menlo Park, Calif.: Institute for the Future, 1979.

Johansen, R., and Samuel, P. *Future Societal Developments and Postsecondary Education: A Handbook for Citizen Organizations.* Menlo Park, Calif.: Institute for the Future, 1977.

Joint Economic Committee on Development. *U.S. Long-Term Economic Growth Prospects Entering a New Era.* Washington, D.C.: Staff Study for Joint Economic Committee Congress, 1978.

Judge, A. (Ed.). *Yearbook of World Problems and Human Potential.* Brussels, Belgium: Mankind 2000, yearly.

Lewis, M. V., and Russell, J. F. *Trends, Events, and Issues Likely to Influence Vocational Education in the 1980s.* Columbus, Ohio: The National Center for Research in Vocational Education, 1981.

Livingstone, D. W. *Organizational Innovativeness: A Conceptual Outline for Comparative Studies.* Toronto: Ontario Institute for Studies in Education, 1970.

Magarrell, J. "Gifts to Higher Education Surpass $3.2 Billion." *Chronicle of Higher Education,* June 9, 1980a, p. 1.

Magarrell, J. "Higher Education Price Index Up a Record 9.9 Percent in Twelve Months." *Chronicle of Higher Education,* Sept. 15, 1980b, p. 14.

Magarrell, J. "Less Money, More Competition for Grants Seen by Foundations." *Chronicle of Higher Education,* Nov. 3, 1980c, p. 1.

Magarrell, J. "State Appropriations Up 19 Percent in One Year, 23 Percent in Two Years." *Chronicle of Higher Education,* Oct. 14, 1980d, p. 7.

Marien, M. *Societal Directions and Alternatives: A Critical Guide to the Literature.* LaFayette, N.Y.: Information for Policy Design, 1976.

Miller, J. W. *Organizational Structure of Nongovernmental Postsecondary Accreditation.* Washington, D.C.: National Commission on Accrediting, 1973.

Millett, J. D. *Higher Education Planning: A Report of Experience and a Forecast of Strategies for Change.* Washington, D.C.: Academy for Educational Development, 1978.

Spence, D. S. *A Profile of Higher Education in the South in 1985.* Atlanta, Ga.: Southern Regional Education Board, 1977.

Spero, I. K. *Government and Higher Education: A Summary of 21 Institutional and Self-Studies.* Cambridge, Mass.: Sloan Commission on Government and Higher Education, 1978.

Utterbach, J. M. "Environmental Analysis and Forecasting." In D. Schendel and and C. Hofer (Eds.), *Strategic Management: A New View of Business Policy and Planning.* Boston: Little, Brown, 1979.

Willingham, W. *A Handbook of Information Sources in Higher Education.* New York: The College Entrance Examination Board, 1973.

Wirtz, W. K. *On Further Examination: Report of the Advisory Panel on SAT Score Decline.* New York: The College Entrance Examination Board, 1977.

Robert H. Glover is director of planning and institutional research at the University of Hartford. Prior to holding this position, he was president of Planned Change Associates, a private consulting firm.

Jeffrey Holmes has recently taken the position of executive director of the Canadian Conference of the Arts. He was previously director of the Education, Science, and Culture Division of Statistics Canada for several years.

The office of institutional research can play a key role in creating an institutional marketing plan. Designing survey instruments and evaluations to support new program development, employer-based education, and recruiting concepts are areas where institutional research can make important contributions.

Research Support for Marketing

John A. Lucas

Chapter Two identified some sources of information about the external environment that can be summarized by institutional researchers for use by institutional planners. There will also be times when a planning activity requires specific information about the external environment that is not available from published reports. This chapter describes several such situations in which institutional researchers need to evaluate one aspect of the external environment—the potential student market.

As competition for students heightens, marketing will gain more acceptance among colleges and universities. Moreover, marketing will have to be well designed and will integrated into the total institutional plan. In most colleges, institutional researchers can be a valuable resource for developing such a marketing effort.

This chapter will focus on the researcher's role in conducting feasibility studies for new program development and in conducting preference surveys for new schedules, new formats, and new courses. Other topics discussed will be the researcher's role in employer-based educational projects, evaluations of brainstorming sessions among common-interest groups, and specific recruiting techniques.

Testing New Programs or Options

One of the most effective ways to attract additional students is to offer new programs or program options. Before an institution can undertake the

N. P. Uhl (Ed.). *Using Research for Strategic Planning.* New Directions for Institutional Research, no. 37. San Francisco: Jossey-Bass, March 1983.

creation of such a new program or option, two basic questions must be answered. First, external agencies such as governing boards want to know what the employment demand is for such a program; or, if such a program leads to graduate or professional degree programs, what their demand is for undergraduates. Second, the institution must know how many additional students will be attracted to such programs. To answer these questions, the office of institutional research can conduct feasibility studies for each proposed program.

Feasibility Studies to Determine the Need for a Program. Employment demand can be determined methodically. The first step will be directed to the proposed target area of employment. This step must be carried out by the program initiator, other interested academic faculty members or administrators, and an advisory committee. The office of institutional research should be present to ensure that basic information is considered, such as the practical geographical limits and the types of employers appropriate for graduates of the proposed program. If targets are graduate or professional schools, a similar procedure would be used and similar information would have to be gathered. A key consideration here would be the number of nearby institutions that have programs similar to the one being proposed.

Next, the institutional research office should determine the mode of sampling. Before this can be determined, however, the researcher must know what kind of return rate can be expected. If the advisory committee has a great many contacts among the target population and can involve them all in the planning process to some extent, then over a 50 percent return can be expected. In this case, a survey population of 500 would be adequate. Thus, only if the target employer population exceeded 500 would the researcher develop a sampling technique. If, however, only a normal number of contacts is available, a researcher can expect only between a 20 and a 30 percent return from an employer population. In this case, the researcher ought to survey the entire target population unless it exceeds 2,000.

If the target population is larger and sampling is desired, there are two approaches that can be used. When an entire target population list can be developed, a systematic sampling technique can be used, whereby every N^{th} employee on the list is selected, until the desired sample size is reached. For example, if the list contained 10,000 names, and the researcher desired a sample of 2,000, every fifth name would be selected. With large populations, complete lists usually take a long time to develop. In this case, a form of stratified sampling could be used. Specifically, a researcher would select a proportionate number of employers representing the geographical regions and the types of employers in the entire population to develop a sample that would proportionately match the population.

After determining the target population and the mode of sampling, the researcher is ready to design the survey instrument. The same academic team that determined the target population can help develop the survey form. The researcher needs first to be a good listener, in order to identify the basic information needed for the study. There is some information that is usually required, such as the number of graduates of the proposed program, whom the firm would hire. Normally, firms can estimate their current requirements, but cannot tell researchers how many graduates would be hired over the next five years. In addition, it is useful to collect information regarding the salaries these graduates would be paid, their expected job titles, and brief job descriptions. Another basic need is to know the number of current employees who would be encouraged to enroll in the program, either to obtain a degree or just to take a few courses. Other information the survey might obtain includes a description of the facilities available for clinical or internship work experiences, available personnel resources, and continuing education needs of the firm. Finally, the survey instrument should be thoroughly reviewed and pretested before being used.

Before the instrument is finalized, the researcher must determine whether the survey will be done through the mail or conducted as an interview. When programs are highly specialized and the sample size is small (under fifty), it is practical and even desirable to have a professional in the field (a faculty member or the program initiator) conduct a structured telephone interview, using the already designed survey instrument. When the target population is large, the only practical means is to conduct a mail survey. A cover letter from the program initiator should accompany the survey instrument.

In the type of survey just described, it is possible to make a conservative estimate of the employment need for the graduates in question. It is also possible to make a partial estimate of student demand for the program by the number of current employees who would enroll. In addition, it is necessary to determine whether enough students would enroll in the program to meet employment needs for new graduates. Usually it is safe to assume that, if the proposed salaries are competitive, the program will be attractive enough to meet employment demands. Enrollment should be controlled so that it does not exceed employment demand. Enrollments based on general interest would not be considered at this stage of the planning process. If proposed salaries are not competitive or if graduates move into graduate or professional schools rather than into employment, then a separate study of potential students would be needed.

Potential Student Surveys. A survey of potential students could be developed by a process very similar to the one used in the employment need survey. The same academic team could first determine the target student potential. Such information as geographical origin and types of students (high school graduates, women returning, and so on) would have to be collected. The mode of sampling also would have to be decided. In this case, a stratified sample, taking representatives from the various geographical origins and types of students, is usually appropriate. The sample size would depend on the specialization of the proposed program and its size. The more specialized, smaller programs would require larger sample sizes to identify those few students who would be interested. Thus, the sample size might vary from several hundred to several thousand.

A survey instrument could then be developed, which would describe the proposed program, give descriptions of likely jobs for graduates of the program, and estimate salaries. Prospective students would be asked to state the likelihood of their enrolling in the new program. If the new program is intended to lead to graduate or professional schools then the students in the survey would be given the names of universities that would accept the new program's degree.

Inferences from Such Studies. In studies determining employment demand and student demand for new academic programs and options, response rates are often low, and the only assumption that can be made is that nonrespondents are not interested in the program. Thus, estimates made with these types of surveys are always on the conservative side. There is another key assumption, however, that has to be made in drawing inferences from the survey data. Employers usually can identify only their present employment needs. Thus, the academic team and the institutional researcher will have to produce a reasonable estimate for the turnover of employment demand. If the present turnover is five years, then the present demand must be spread over a five-year period. This kind of assumption will help prevent any new program from oversaturating the market in a short period of time.

Pitfalls. The most common problem occurs when the description of the new program or option is unclear to prospective employers and they are unable to say whether or not they would hire the proposed graduates. The role of an advisory committee can be crucial in avoiding this error. Another pitfall occurs when cautions in making inferences are not observed, as described previously. Still another pitfall can occur in selecting the target area for employers. If the area chosen is too large, unaccounted-for competitors in education will diminish the need for the proposed program. Thus, any survey estimates of employment demand would be inflated. Also, if the geographical area is too large, other factors might have to be considered, such as willingness of students to travel to the institution for the new program and their willingness to accept employment at a distance. If the target area chosen is too small, the new program may be rejected for lack of anticipated enrollments, when in fact there would be adequate demand for the program from a wider target area.

Interrelationship with Planning. Surveys of employment demand and potential student demand related to the planning process in several ways. First, these surveys provide enrollment estimates for the new programs, which feed into the total enrollment projection format for the institution. Second, the enrollment estimates provide cost estimates for the proposed programs, which feed in turn into the budgeting process. Most important, the very process of developing and conducting a survey can become an integral part of the orderly process of considering new program options within the total planning framework of the institution.

Testing Other Academic Variables

In the course of curriculum evaluation, often it is suggested to try new courses or new formats or to try to serve a different clientele. In some cases, new courses or formats may be suggested for the present student body. Surveys can be designed to test in advance whether new clientele can be attracted to existing programs or whether current students would benefit from a modification in the curriculum. This advance knowledge allows academic personnel to concentrate their efforts for curriculum modification or recruiting in specific areas, which have a high probability of succeeding. Data from these surveys are easier to interpret than the new program feasibility studies described previously, because current experience with enrollments in the target curriculum is available and can act as a basis of comparison for all other tests of modifications. Equally important is the availability of faculty and staff members who are familiar with the target program being modified.

If new as well as old clientele are to be served by an existing program, the new group should be sampled in a survey. In this case, the survey instrument should determine what the college should do differently to attract the new clientele. The instrument could include both existing course descriptions and proposed new course descriptions. If the present course descriptions are preferred, then new courses are unlikely to attract the new clientele. The sample could also be presented with different formats, such as weekend schedules, two-week concentrated offerings, or different teaching methods. Again, if existing formats are preferred to the proposed new formats, then new formats will be unlikely to attract the new clientele. Many times this new clientele may consist of persons employed in the curriculum field who simply need additional training to upgrade their skills. The same kinds of surveys can be conducted among current students to see if new courses or new formats are especially attractive to them. This procedure could result in current students' taking heavier loads or remaining longer at the institution to enroll in additional offerings.

Unlike new program feasibility studies, low return rates on these new course or format preference studies present special problems; there is no valid assumption to use in making inferences from the data. The best one can do is infer that the entire population would have the same preferences as the sample of respondents. This is not likely, but there is no way of knowing in which direction a bias will appear. For current students, it is a rather simple process to attain at least an 80 percent return rate and thus avoid any significant bias. Samples among potential new clientele, however, will almost always result in low return rates and probable bias. Another pitfall of these preference studies could be inadequate descriptions of the new courses and formats. Testing these other academic variables can be an integral part of the curriculum evaluation process, as well as a part of the enrollment projection process.

Exploring the Need for Employer-Based Programs

This chapter has been exploring ways in which institutional researchers can help institutions attract students. In this section, we shall look at a way in which a researcher can help bring the institution to the client. Employer-based programs are probably most likely to lead to enrollment increases in the next ten years, but they are probably also the concept colleges are least prepared to implement.

Surveys are not useful in determining need for employer-based programs. These programs are so complex and individually tailored that several client conferences are required to explain and negotiate a plan of action. Moreover, in most cases the potential demand is far beyond most colleges' capacity to satisfy. Thus, instead of using surveys, the effort is initiated with several pilot projects. As in a program feasibility study, an academic team including the institutional researcher will be required.

Educational Needs Assessment. The cornerstone of an effective employer-based program is a well-conceived needs assessment. Firms interested in such programs usually are vague about their needs. A needs assessment can sharpen their ideas and produce a clear educational plan.

The needs assessment process starts with interviews of top managers and outlines the general educational needs of the target employees. Then, structured interviews are held with sample groups of the targeted employees. These interviews identify the education and training needed to meet the employees' perceived organizational and personal goals. Survey forms are then designed to include these perceived needs and are given either to the entire population or to a larger sample of the targeted employees in order to verify the ideas generated in the interviews.

The academic team will then package a series of courses and seminars to meet these needs. In most cases, these will be from existing offerings, but sometimes new courses and seminars will have to be developed. This educational plan, which also includes the organizational objectives to be achieved, will be presented for final approval to the top management of the firm. This needs assessment process will be carried out for each interested organization, although it is better to start with just a few pilot projects.

Role of the Institutional Researcher. The role of the institutional researcher is twofold in this case. First, this person can be very valuable in designing the structured interview and the individual survey forms and in interpreting the results. Second, the researcher can help structure the evaluation of each project. At least every two years, an evaluation should determine to what extent organizational objectives have been met and what modifications need to be made. This evaluation should be reviewed with the top management of the firm. The evaluation should focus on what students learned and on resources required to maintain the program. Learning can be assessed by surveying students and their work supervisors. The survey instrument could determine the extent to which students increased their skills or job knowledge or gained new motivation or new perspectives as a result of the educational program. These questions should closely reflect the original goals set for the program.

Faculty members involved in the program, in consultation with the management of the firm, can assess the future potential for employee enrollment in the program. Should the program be curtailed, kept at its present level, or expanded? An assessment should be made to determine whether there are enough qualified faculty members to expand the program, either at the pilot firm or at other firms, if requested. Faculty members should evaluate facilities and support services. Finally, there should be a clear accounting of all revenues derived from the program and all costs incurred, including support services and administration.

Pitfalls in Employer-Based Pilot Projects. The single biggest pitfall here is eagerness to jump to conclusions as a result of a successful pilot study. One must be very cautious in these cases. Pilot studies may be very successful for two basic reasons, either of which would not warrant a recommendation for expansion. First, the early projects may be successful because the college's most qualified staff and faculty members are conducting the needs assessment and organizing the educational programs. Frequently, colleges have few staff and faculty members who are qualified to work in this area. This limitation can be overcome partially by using pilot projects to train inexperienced faculty and staff members. The second reason for early success can center around the selection process. Early projects often involve firms that already have close ties to the college, and these are often the projects most likely to succeed.

Another pitfall is too much publicity. It is almost imperative in these cases to keep a low profile, as the potential demand is usually beyond the college's ability to provide services.

Planning Issues. There are two key planning issues that will determine the future growth of employer-based education. These issues must be addressed in the college's long-range plan and financial plan. The first issue involves the extent to which the college is willing to invest in staff members to coordinate the entire project. Solutions could range from arranging an overload for one staff member to hiring a full-time staff coordinator and several full-time staff members. The second issue involves the college's willingness to invest in released time for the training of inexperienced faculty and staff members, to allow for the program's future growth.

Providing Research Aid for Other Student Recruiting Programs

As with employer-based educational programs, there are other situations where surveys alone may not be adequate to assess needs — for example, when assessing needs among special-interest groups such as senior citizens, reentry women, community leaders, and so forth. In many cases, a series of brainstorming sessions may be required to help potential students identify their needs and recognize how the college might satisfy them. Researchers can be of real help in evaluating these sessions. While brainstorming can identify many needs, the process often is not cost effective; thus, evalution is essential. The evaluation should consider the number and quality of the ideas generated during the brainstorming process. In addition, the evaluation should seek answers to questions such as the following: Can the nucleus of an enthusiastic planning and advisory committee be identified for the proposed program? Were enough potential students identified to make the proposed program feasible? Can the time and staff required to organize and run the brainstorming sessions be justified by the future potential of the proposed program?

Another area in which researchers can help is in evaluating continuing recruiting efforts. For example, the admissions office can be evaluated by examining relationships among inquiries, applications, acceptances, and eventual enrollment. Valuable information for recruitment packages can also be obtained from follow-up studies of alumni. Such studies should include information concerning present status, current education, and occupation. For example, if alumni are continuing their education, the study should be designed to find out where they are enrolled and how they are performing. If they are employed, the study should find out what jobs they are performing, their salaries, places of employment, and how well they believe they were prepared for their jobs.

Finally, there is the concept of a total, comprehensive needs assessment. This type of assessment usually refers to the sampling from a total population of all possible employers, as well as to continuing education opportunities for graduates of the target institution. The desired outcome is a priority listing of all the new program development and curriculum revision needs for the college. While this is an admirable goal, such a project may well exceed the scope of an institutional research office and may require the help of outside agencies, as well as the total involvement of the college staff. The inordinate amount of effort required may not be repaid by the results. This topic is discussed in more detail in an earlier work by Lucas (1974).

Reference

Lucas, J. A. "Marketing Analysis of Proposed New Programs in a Growing Community College." *Research Series,* 1974, *5,* 10.

John A. Lucas has been director of planning and institutional research at William Rainey Harper College in Palatine, Illinois, since 1969.

Evaluations must be relevant, accurate, credible, timely, and persuasive for maximum impact on strategic planning.

Academic Program Evaluation

Mary Jo Clark

As noted in the first chapter of this sourcebook, academic program review or evaluation is only one part of institutional assessment for strategic planning. Nevertheless, it is often considered a key element in the evaluation of institutional strengths and weaknesses, since it focuses attention on the performance of individual degree programs, departments, or other academic units such as schools, colleges, or off-campus centers. Narrowing attention in this way is particularly helpful when the evaluation results are to be linked with the planning process.

The term *evaluation* implies value judgments about the strengths and weaknesses of academic programs and, in addition, provides descriptive information about them. The kinds of information collected and the ways in which the data are summarized and interpreted will depend in large part on the purposes for conducting the review, the anticipated ways the results will be used, and the characteristics of the program to be reviewed. For example, the design of program reviews will vary somewhat, depending on whether the focus is on a department of physics or on a department of French and on whether the setting is a small undergraduate college or a large, complex university. Reviews for internal planning and program improvement will differ from those mandated by accrediting agencies or state coordinating boards. Thus, it is easier to talk about the principles of conducting academic program evaluations than to describe specific ways for carrying out such evaluations. This chapter reviews some of the recent literature on the topic, including case study reports of the

N. P. Uhl (Ed.). *Using Research for Strategic Planning.* New Directions for Institutional Research, no. 37. San Francisco: Jossey-Bass, March 1983.

ways in which systematic reviews of programs have been designed and carried out at selected colleges and universities. Particular attention is given to descriptions and evaluations of the procedures that have been used or suggested for collecting information.

Models and Procedures for Academic Program Evaluation

Considerable diversity in the design and conducting of academic program reviews has been identified in recent literature. Good reviews of the historical background, conceptual issues, alternative evaluation strategies, and design options can be found in Craven (1980a and 1980b), Dressel (1976), Feasley (1980), Mims (1978), and Wilson (1982). Davis and Dougherty (1979) and Shirley and Volkwein (1978) specifically address problems in the design of review procedures that may lead to the reallocation of resources among academic programs. Penny (1981, pp. 93–94) reproduces a set of questions that Yale's provost would ask about any academic activity being evaluated. Mortimer and Tierney (1979, pp. 57–61) include checklists for academic quality assessment and program evaluation. Craven (1980a, pp. 444–449) poses a series of questions that should be answered in designing and implementing an effective evaluation system. Lehmann (1981, pp. 766–770) makes six recomendations to colleges that are just beginning evaluation studies and are concerned about ways to integrate them successfully within the planning cycle.

Although many different perspectives are represented in the above materials, most of the authors would agree that a fundamental reason for reviewing academic programs is to collect information that can be used to make judgments about a program's quality or value. To be useful for this purpose, the information that is collected must be relevant, accurate, credible, timely, and persuasive. The old circular system of *why–who–when–what* can be helpful in the planning process:

1. Why conduct program reviews? What questions need to be answered? There is no single model or best way, but there are guidelines and resources available to those who have clear ideas about what they hope to accomplish.

2. Who will be involved? Primary responsibility for deciding to carry out reviews, approving the overall design, and making use of the results generally resides with a chief academic officer or a director of planning. The specifics of the design, data collection and analysis, and preparation of reports frequently will be the responsibility of institutional researchers. In many respects, internal review is a political process; it requires the commitment of leaders in key positions and the involvement of representatives from all the various constituencies, including, particularly, faculty members and students in the programs under review.

3. When should the review take place? The schedule will be influenced by the date when results are needed and by competing demands on the time of those most closely involved. These time constraints will in turn influence decisions about the kinds of information that will be sought, since various procedures require different amounts of time. Reviews are of little value if decisions must be made before the results are available.

4. What kinds of information should be collected? Reviews of specific data-collection procedures are presented in the next section of this chapter. Decisions about the best procedures to use in any given situation will depend on the purposes of the review, the characteristics of the program to be reviewed, and the time and money available to carry out the review. The procedures for data collection must be appropriate to the criteria that will be used to make judgments about the program. Whatever the details, care must be taken to make sure that the process involves representatives of the various groups that will be affected, treats each group fairly, and includes a variety of measures or indicators to reflect different dimensions of the program.

5. Why were the data collected, and how can they be useful in making decisions and in planning for the future of the program or the institution? The cycle of questions comes full circle with use of the results.

Assessing Program Quality

Good general discussions of various methods that might be used in the assessment of educational quality are provided by Dressel (1976), Stauffer (1981), and Webster (1981). A variety of checklists, questionnaires, tests, and other assessment procedures are included in these sources and in references that follow below. The most frequent form of data collection, the program or departmental self-study, will be discussed first, followed by a review of some possible ways to assess learning outcomes of students and scholarly contributions of the faculty. Finally, reputational ratings of program quality are considered briefly.

Program Self-Study. In a recent survey, more than 450 heads of university departments reported on the purposes, number, and content of recent program reviews conducted by their departments (Clark, 1977). Most of the departments had conducted three or more reviews in the past ten years. Approximately 40 percent of the most recent reviews were conducted primarily to provide information for departmental use; another 40 percent focused primarily on information for outside groups such as professional accreditation committees or state coordinating agencies. Frequently collected information included descriptive data about faculty training and publications, program resources, and course enrollments; student evaluations of courses; and student and faculty judgments about the quality of various program elements. Notably absent were measures of what was learned in the program, explanations of why some students dropped out, and reports on the activities and opinions of program graduates. Most respondents thought more survey data from faculty members, students, and graduates would be helpful as a part of internally initiated reviews.

The procedures of self-studies are described in some detail in *A Handbook for Self-Assessment* (State University of New York, 1979), Kells (1980), and Tritschler (1981). Ways to review and evaluate teaching are summarized in Centra (1977). Data about enrollments, degrees, and cost should be available in the institution's management information system and can be used as part of a review. Several questionnaires have been developed for use in the assessment of program processes, such as environment for learning, faculty–student relationships, and management, and in the assessment of student and faculty activities and satisfaction with programs. The environmental assessment techniques are discussed in some detail by Baird and Hartnett (1980). Gray and others (1979) provide computer-ready questionnaires that can be used to survey undergraduates at various points, from entry to recent-alumni status. Survey questionnaires for use in the review of graduate programs are provided by the *Graduate Program Self-Assessment Service* (Clark, 1980). Evidence concerning the value of alumni surveys is provided by Wise, Hengstler, and Braskamp (1981). A program review strategy that focuses particularly on relating costs to academic program performance is described in some detail by Lehmann (1981, pp. 757–766). Systematic procedures for data collection of the kinds provided by the questionnaires described in these references can save time and money for individual institutions, make it possible to compare results across programs, and help develop relationships between review results and planning processes.

Most of the above-mentioned assessment procedures, despite being frequently labeled as measures of program outcomes, are concerned primarily with program processes, rather than with results or effectiveness. Although there are conceptual as well as methodological problems, most authors urge more attention to the measurement of outcomes when academic programs are being evaluated.

Assessing Student Learning. Much of the literature on the measurement of educational outcomes emphasizes tests of subject matter content, the development of skills and critical thinking, and the ability to apply knowledge. Some programs also are interested in the extent to which they have influenced student interests, values, and citizenship. Pace (1979) summarizes findings from higher education outcomes studies from the 1930s to the 1970s in sections on the assessment of undergraduate achievement during college, evidence concerning the achievements of program graduates, and studies of institutional effects. Astin (1977) gives special attention to methodological issues in college-impact research and analysis. Lehmann (1981) reviews several tests that have been used or are being developed to assess learning in programs of general education, discipline specialization, and professional training. One of these studies (Whitla, 1977) is concerned particularly with value-added assessment in liberal education programs. A good summary of the problems involved in the comparative assessment of student outcomes in higher education can be found in Hartnett (1974). Principles and guidelines for designing program reviews that will identify and measure educational outcomes are provided by Ball (1981, pp. 72–79), Baugher (1981, pp. 101–105), and Bowen (1979, pp. 22–26).

These discussions of self-studies and outcomes assessment have been concerned primarily with ways to obtain quantified information about academic programs. Braskamp (1982, pp. 59–61) makes a strong case for including implicit criteria and standards in evaluation systems, as well as for including explicit criteria that lend themselves to quantifiable indicators or measures. He cites four limitations of quantitative indicators: (1) Although psychometrically sound, the data may lack credibility with users; (2) a limited number of measures may not adequately reflect the unique features of the program being evaluated; (3) using quantitative measures in decision making may bring about undesirable changes in the characteristic being measured (for example, the use of credit hours in resource allocation is likely to create attempts to generate more credit hours); and (4) centralized or standardized approaches reduce the role of faculty members and peers in the process. Instead of depending heavily on quantitative data to organize a program review, Braskamp advocates the use of issues (salient and important matters that need attention) and concerns (disagreements about matters by relevant constituencies). He notes that this approach may be especially beneficial for linking evaluation with planning, since problems and future aspirations unique to a program receive more attention.

Assessing Faculty Scholarship. Considerable attention has been given in recent literature to ways of measuring the scholarly productivity of faculty members who are associated with a given program or department. In general, these procedures are of more interest in the assessment of graduate degree programs than at the undergraduate level. An excellent review of these procedures and their strengths and weaknesses is provided by Jones (1980), where quantitative and qualitative assessments of publications and the use of citation indexes are discussed in depth. A variety of other measures are reviewed more briefly, such as the number of awards or research grants. The unique problems of evaluating scholarship in the performing arts and in clinical services are also discussed.

Reputational Ratings. Global ratings of the quality of academic programs are sometimes made by the authors of educational guidebooks, as well as by educational experts who are rating programs in their own disciplines or professional specializations. Lawrence and Green (1980) provide a good summary and critique of this method of assessing program quality. Reputational rating procedures have been used most extensively at the graduate level, but also have been tried recently at the undergraduate level by Astin and Solmon

(1981). The most appealing feature of reputational ratings—and, at the same time, their greatest weakness—is in the unitary nature of the measure. A number of studies have examined the correlates of program quality, as rated by relevant experts, emphasizing the importance of multiple measures to reflect the diversity and complexity of most academic programs (see, for example, Clark, Hartnett, and Baird, 1976).

Using Evaluative Data in Planning

The data collected as part of an academic program review must be relevant, credible, accurate, timely, and persuasive. Without these characteristics, the data will not be used. Assessment is the activity that links the evaluation and planning processes, as depicted in Figure 1. Continuity of the planning cycle depends on the feedback of information developed through the specification of program goals, measures of program processes and outcomes, and comparison with previous conditions or with some other standard. The circular relationship of the evaluation and planning processes emphasizes the continuous nature of both activities.

Poulton (1978) reviews the ways in which evaluations of academic programs are used at various organizational levels and identifies factors in the organizational environment that influence the use of program reviews. Davis and Dougherty (1979), Mortimer and Tierney (1979), and Shirley and Volkwein (1978) present specific examples of ways in which data from program re-

Figure 1. Interlocking Planning and Evaluation Cycles

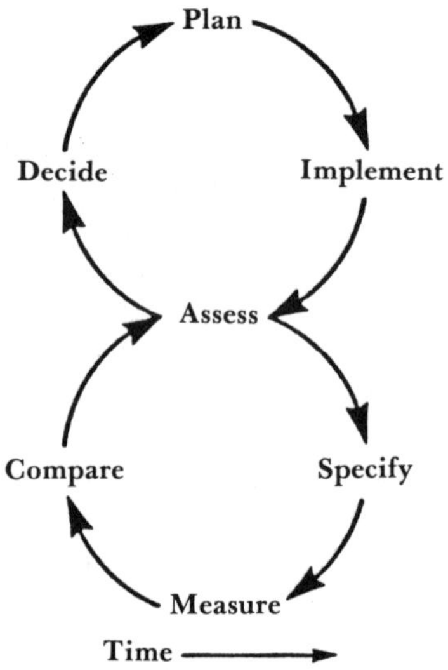

Plan
Decide
Implement
Assess
Compare
Specify
Measure
Time

Source: Chickering and Associates, 1981, p. 751.

views have been or could be used to set program priorities or reallocate resources among departments. Using data comparatively — whether for comparing this year's data with earlier information about the same program or for using standard measures to collect information about different programs within or across universities — is discussed by Clark (1980). A collection of essays edited by Braskamp and Brown (1980) considers broad issues related to the use of evaluative information, including ways to present results effectively. Their monograph concludes with a utilization enhancement checklist (pp. 94–97) that would benefit anyone involved in planning for or carrying out reviews of academic programs.

Case Study Reports of Program Reviews

No extensive search for reports of individual institutional practices was undertaken as a part of preparing this chapter, but descriptions of program review activities on the following campuses can be found in the materials cited below:

- Several campuses at the State University of New York: *A Handbook for Self-Assessment* (1979) and Tritschler (1981)
- Florida institutions: Feasley (1980)
- University of Illinois: Wilson (1982)
- University of Michigan: Davis and Dougherty (1979)
- Michigan State University, University of Michigan, and University of Houston: Craven (1980b)
- Ohio State University and the University of Vermont: Arns and Poland (1980)
- State Colleges and Universities of Pennsylvania: Mortimer and Tierney (1979)
- University of Wisconsin: Craven (1980a).

If more evidence is needed, these reports will make it clear that no one evaluation plan is appropriate for all purposes or places. Perhaps the main value of these case studies is their emphasis on the importance of collaborative planning for program review, their descriptions of political sensitivities uncovered in the process of conducting reviews, and reports of experience in developing and using various data-collection procedures. Although it is seldom possible to transplant a program review system from one institution to another, there is much that can be learned from the work that has already been done. The principles, guidelines, checklists, questionnaires, and recommendations summarized in recent publications are important aids to more thoughtful, comprehensive, and useful academic program evaluations.

Program Evaluation and Strategic Planning

A few years ago, the Council of Graduate Schools and the Graduate Record Examinations Board sponsored a survey of graduate deans to identify the kinds of information that should be collected in assessing the quality of graduate programs, the acceptability of various methods of data collection, and the ways in which the results could be used in planning (see Clark, 1980; Clark, Hartnett, and Baird, 1976). Although focused on graduate education, the characteristics and indicators that were identified are relevant also to the evaluation of academic programs at other levels. Interestingly, the deans endorsed the use of self-reports and judgments by faculty members, enrolled students, and recent alumni as indicators of program status on many of the following dimensions:

Program Resources

1. History, reputation, current purposes, and goals
2. Faculty academic training
3. Faculty research and scholarly activity
4. Attractiveness to students; student academic ability at entrance
5. Financial support (internal and external)
6. Library and other scholarly resources
7. Physical facilities

Program Processes

8. Course and program offerings
9. Faculty teaching effectiveness
10. Faculty concern for student development and welfare
11. Faculty and student involvement in program affairs
12. Faculty and student morale
13. Faculty and student satisfaction with learning environment, departmental policies and procedures, departmental leadership, assistantship and internship experiences, evaluation of student progress toward degree completion
14. Student academic commitment and motivation
15. Admissions processes, retention, and rate of degree completion
16. Relationships with cognate programs
17. Environment for faculty teaching and research

Program Outcomes

18. Student achievement, knowledge, and skills at time of degree completion
19. Faculty research and scholarly productivity
20. Job placement of graduates
21. Professional accomplishments of graduates
22. Alumni assessments of educational experiences

Research on the dimensions of quality in graduate education demonstrated that reliable indicators of many of these important program characteristics were available from departmental records, self-reports of program participants, or judgments based on personal observation. The measures could be arranged in turn to provide a profile of program performance on a variety of dimensions, and the use of common data-collection procedures permitted the comparison of profiles across programs. The profiles of results provided a convenient way to summarize self-study information for use in program improvement, institutional decisions about the allocation of resources, and longer-term strategic planning. Academic programs at other levels could develop similar profiles of performance by identifying the program characteristics most important for their levels and types, using available data-collection procedures or developing their own, and establishing cooperative arrangements with similar programs to provide comparison data.

References

Arns, R. G., and Poland, W. "Changing the University Through Program Review." *Journal of Higher Education,* 1980, *51,* 268–284.

Astin, A. W. *Four Critical Years: Effects of College on Beliefs, Attitudes, and Knowledge.* San Francisco: Jossey-Bass, 1977.

Astin, A. W., and Solmon, L. C. "The Quality of Undergraduate Education: Are Reputational Ratings Needed to Measure Quality?" *Change,* September 1981, *13* (6), 23–28, and October 1981, *13* (7), 14–19.

Baird, C. C., and Hartnett, R. T. *Understanding Student and Faculty Life.* San Francisco: Jossey-Bass, 1980.

Ball, S. (Ed.). *New Directions for Program Evaluation: Assessing and Interpreting Outcomes,* no. 9. San Francisco: Jossey-Bass, 1981.

Baugher, D. (Ed.). *New Directions for Program Evaluation: Measuring Effectiveness,* no. 11. San Francisco: Jossey-Bass, 1981.

Bowen, H. R. "Goals, Outcomes, and Academic Evaluation." In *Evaluating Educational Quality: A Conference Summary.* Washington, D.C.: : The Council on Postsecondary Accreditation, 1979.

Braskamp, L. A. "Evaluation Systems Are More Than Information Systems." In R. F. Wilson (Ed.), *New Directions for Higher Education: Designing Academic Program Reviews,* no. 37. San Francisco: Jossey-Bass, 1982.

Braskamp, L. A., and Brown, R. D. (Eds.). *New Directions for Program Evaluation: Utilization of Evaluative Information,* no. 5. San Francisco: Jossey-Bass, 1980.

Centra, J. A. (Ed.). *New Directions for Higher Education: Reviewing and Evaluating Teaching,* no. 17. San Francisco: Jossey-Bass, 1977.

Chickering, A., and Associates. *The Modern American College.* San Francisco: Jossey-Bass, 1981.

Clark, M. J. *Program Review Practices of University Departments.* Princeton, N.J.: Educational Testing Service, 1977.

Clark, M. J. *Graduate Program Self-Assessment Service: Handbook for Users.* Princeton, N.J.: Educational Testing Service, 1980.

Clark, M. J., Hartnett, R. T., and Baird, L. L. *Assessing Dimensions of Quality in Doctoral Education: A Technical Report of a National Study in Three Fields.* Princeton, N.J.: Educational Testing Service, 1976.

Craven, E. C. "Evaluating Program Performance." In P. Jedamus, M. N. Peterson, and Associates (Eds.). *Improving Academic Management: A Handbook of Planning and Institutional Research.* San Francisco: Jossey-Bass, 1980a.

Craven, E. C. (Ed.). *New Directions for Institutional Research: Alternative Models of Academic Program Evaluation,* no. 27. San Francisco: Jossey-Bass, 1980b.

Davis, C. K., and Dougherty, E. A. "Guidelines for Program Discontinuance." *Educational Record,* Winter 1979, pp. 68–77.

Dressel, P. L. *Handbook for Academic Evaluation: Assessing Institutional Effectiveness, Student Progress, and Professional Performance for Decision Making in Higher Education.* San Francisco: Jossey-Bass, 1976.

Feasley, C. E. *Program Evaluation.* AAHE-ERIC/Higher Education Research Report No. 2. Washington, D.C.: American Association for Higher Education, 1980.

Gray, R. G., and others. *Student Outcomes Questionnaires: An Implementation Handbook.* Boulder, Colo.: National Center for Higher Education Management Systems, 1979.

Hartnett, R. T. *Problems with the Comparative Assessment of Student Outcomes in Higher Education.* Princeton, N.J.: Educational Testing Service, 1974.

Jones, L. V. "The Assessment of Scholarship." In E. Loveland (Ed.), *New Directions for Program Evaluation: Measuring the Hard-to-Measure,* no. 6. San Francisco: Jossey-Bass, 1980.

Kells, H. R. *Self-Study Processes: A Guide for Postsecondary Institutions.* Washington, D.C.: American Council on Education, 1980.

Lawrence, J. K., and Green, K. C. *The Higher Education Rating Game: A Question of Quality.* ERIC/Higher Education Research Report No. 5. Washington, D.C.: American Association for Higher Education, 1980.

Lehmann, T. "Evaluating Adult Learning and Program Costs." In A. Chickering (Ed.), *The Modern American College: Responding to the New Students and a Changing Society.* San Francisco: Jossey-Bass, 1981.

Mims, R. S. "Program Review and Evaluation: Designing and Implementing the Review Process." Paper presented at the annual meeting of the Association for Institutional Research, Houston, 1978.

Mortimer, K. P., and Tierney, M. L. *The Three "Rs" of the Eighties: Reduction, Reallocation, and Retrenchment.* AAHE-ERIC/Higher Education Research Report No. 4. Washington, D.C.: American Association for Higher Education, 1979.

Pace, C. R. *Assessing College Outcomes.* San Francisco: Jossey-Bass, 1979.

Penny, S. H. "Evaluation for Action." In T. M. Stauffer (Ed.), *Quality — Higher Education's Principal Challenge.* Washington, D.C.: American Council on Education, 1981.

Poulton, N. L. "Program Review and Evaluation: Integrating Results into Decision Making." Paper presented at the annual meeting of the Association for Institutional Research, Houston, 1978.

Shirley, R. C., and Volkwein, J. F. "Establishing Academic Program Priorities." *Journal of Higher Education,* 1978, *49* (5), 472–488.

State University of New York. *A Handbook for Self-Assessment.* Albany, N.Y.: State University of New York, 1979.

Stauffer, T. M. (Ed.). *Quality — Higher Education's Principal Challenge.* Washington, D.C.: American Council on Education, 1981.

Tritschler, D. "Strategies for Assessing Performance at Your Own Institution." In R. I. Miller (Ed.), *New Directions for Institutional Research: Institutional Assessment for Self-Improvement,* no. 2. San Francisco: Jossey-Bass, 1981.

Webster, D. S. "Methods of Assessing Quality: Advantages and Disadvantages." *Change,* 1981, *13* (7), 20–24.

Whitla, D. K. *Value Added: Measuring the Outcomes of Undergraduate Education.* Cambridge, Mass.: Harvard University Press, 1977.

Wilson, R. F. (Ed.). *New Directions for Higher Education: Designing Academic Program Reviews,* no. 37. San Francisco: Jossey-Bass, 1982.

Wise, S. L., Hengstler, D. D., and Braskamp, L. A. "Alumni Ratings as an Indicator of Departmental Quality." *Journal of Educational Psychology,* 1981, *73,* 71-77.

Mary Jo Clark is a research psychologist at Educational Testing Service in Princeton, New Jersey. Her recent research has been in academic program review, the assessment of educational outcomes, and the problems of special populations such as older students, women, and minorities in higher education.

Facilities analysis provides an important input to planning.
Its methodology is discussed here, as well as how it can be used in planning.

Facilities Analysis: A Tool in Strategic Planning

Charles L. Wheeler

Facilities Analysis: What and Why?

A *facility* may be defined as any physical structure that an institution requires for its programs and related activities. The term includes parking areas,
buildings, parks, rooms, service areas, agricultural fields, outdoor playing
fields, and landscaped areas. For the purposes of this chapter, however, the
definition of *facilities* will be limited to buildings and their interior spaces.
Facilities analysis, therefore, will comprise an examination of a higher education complex, its buildings, and their relations in the systematic self-appraisal
of the present and future competence of the institution and its ability to perform its mission. Facilities analysis results in statements of the institution's
strengths and limitations, which later may be considered as information in the
strategic planning process.

Higher education institutions need to coordinate a variety of personnel, financial, physical plant, and equipment resources to achieve their goals
and objectives. Facilities analysis provides one body of information essential to
this process. Although buildings do not represent the most important resource
of an institution, they do play an important role in higher education. Buildings house the programs of institutions, and the amount and types of space
available may affect the quality and even limit the scope of institutional programs. Maintenance of inappropriate facilities may drain the resources of an

N. P. Uhl (Ed.). *Using Research for Strategic Planning.* New Directions for
Institutional Research, no. 37. San Francisco: Jossey-Bass, March 1983.

institution, just as the acquisition of physical facilities represents a major commitment of current and projected financial resources and may define or constrain program offerings for a considerable period. The appearance of facilities also is a major factor in an institution's image.

What are the different methods and techniques available to perform facilities analysis, and what are their strengths and weaknesses? All methods and techniques for facilities analysis of which this author is aware depend in the first place on the completion and availability of a facilities inventory for the institution. Various standards are then applied to assess how efficiently the facilities are being used.

Review of Literature. In contrast, perhaps, with the literature in many other areas in which institutional researchers work, the literature that must be mastered to conduct facilities analysis is limited and coherent. This section will describe the references with which institutional researchers should be familiar, assess the strengths and weaknesses of the approaches suggested, and outline how this body of thinking evolved. Inventory and assessment procedures will be described in more detail in subsequent sections of this chapter.

Bareither and Schillinger's *University Space Planning* (1968) is especially useful, in that it describes concisely an inventory of facilities, a technique for analysis, and the manner in which the analysis is used in facilities planning. Other works providing additional detail about inventory and assessment procedures include the following: The *Facilities Inventory and Classification Manual, 1973* (Romney, 1974) provides all the information essential to conducting the inventory and classifying space on a programmatic basis. The *Higher Education Facilities Planning and Management Manuals* (Dahnke and others, 1971) describe procedures for facilities analysis using the data compiled in the inventory. This publication is a series of seven separately bound volumes. *Manual One* is an overview of facilities planning and management, *Manual Two* gives detailed procedures for analyzing classroom and class laboratory facilities, and *Manual Three* provides similar information for office and research facilities, while *Manual Four* covers academic support facilities. *Manual Five* deals with the assessment of general support facilities, *Manual Six* describes how institutional program planning and analysis data are used in facilities planning, and *Manual Seven* is a reference guide containing a glossary, an index, and an extensive bibliography. Finally, *Federal Support for Higher Education Construction: Current Programs and Future Needs* (Norris, 1969) uses broad normative measures of square feet of academic space per full-time equivalent (FTE) student by type and level of institution for facilities analysis on a nationwide basis. This approach is useful also for statewide studies and for systems of higher education.

The major strength of the procedures described in the publications cited above is that they provide excellent coverage of most of the facilities of an institution of higher education. These procedures tell the institution what space is available and how effectively it is being used. The major shortcoming of these procedures is that coverage of the system is incomplete. As noted above, facilities analysis accounts for buildings and their interior spaces. Parking lots, outdoor playing fields, parks, agricultural fields, landscaped areas, and other types of exterior spaces are not included, although they are essential facilities.

The system of facilities analysis does not provide information on the condition of space or on its adequacy for present use. The system can be expanded readily to include these data, but the process poses certain problems in procuring consistent data. Experience has demonstrated that institutional personnel often hold highly subjective views regarding the condition and adequacy of space. The services of architects and engineers can be used to arrive at more objective and uniform ratings of space, but this process involves considerable expense.

Also, no two institutions of higher education are identical. Standards for using space are based largely on normative practices. Conceivably, an institution may be so different from other institutions that normative standards will not apply. This author is convinced, however, that the burden of proof in the facilities planning process should be on the institution to demonstrate such a degree of difference.

We have already noted that the literature regarding facilities analysis is relatively limited and coherent. A brief review of this literature's development will explain this fact. While rudimentary forms of space management and projection have always been practiced by colleges and universities, only in the period following World War II were fairly uniform terms and procedures developed (Bareither, 1981). The first major analytical study in this area to receive national circulation was the 1957 *Manual for Studies of Space Utilization in Colleges and Universities* (Russell and Doi, 1957). Another early work was that of McConnell, Holy, and Semans (1955), which established space and space-use standards for public higher education institutions in California. These standards were widely adopted by other states as the interest in facilities planning grew.

The tremendous amount of new construction needed to accommodate post-World War II enrollment created a major incentive for more sophisticated planning. The enactment of the Higher Education Facilities Act of 1963 and its implementation by the U.S. Office of Education also encouraged the development of comparative standards based on uniform methods of analyzing and classifying physical facilities. Substantial federal support became available for the construction of academic facilities, and the regulations required that state higher education facilities commissions establish priority rankings for project applications, based on objective and measurable criteria. In 1966, Congress made funds available to the state commission so that comprehensive facilities-planning studies could be undertaken. In most states, the initial effort was to complete a comprehensive space inventory and utilization survey covering all institutions of higher education in the state (Wheeler, 1969). Also in 1966, a committee under the auspices of the National Center for Educational Statistics began preparing the *Higher Education Facilities Classification and Inventory Procedures Manuals,* designed to be consistent with the best institutional practices and procedures and to serve as a guideline for national practice. This committee, composed of nearly thirty persons, constituted a veritable *Who's Who* of facilities planners at the national, state, and institutional levels. Official publication of the *Manual* was in 1968 (Osso, 1968). This manual was the primary basis of establishing inventories in each of the fifty states and for generating the first national and comparable state totals of various types of facilities. As a result of this experience, a revised version of the *Manual* appeared in 1974 (Romney, 1974). By this time, uniform procedures had been established for space, program, and building classification throughout the federal and state agencies, as well as in higher education institutions.

In summary, the federal Higher Education Facilities Act, by requiring that grants be awarded on the basis of objective criteria, accelerated the development of facilities analysis doctrine. The federal education agencies then took the initiative in bringing together virtually all the major facilities planners to develop the policy documents. As a result, consensus was achieved on a great many points where divergent procedures might otherwise have developed.

The Building Inventory. The building inventory is a tabulation of all buildings and rooms at an institution. It uses classification systems, codes, and definitions necessary for describing and quantifying building areas in terms of the statistical aggregations useful for planning at all levels of resource allocation. A detailed description of inventory procedures is beyond the scope of this chapter, but readers who want to know more details about these procedures may consult Romney (1974) and Bareither and Schillinger (1968).

The building inventory serves a number of important purposes. It can be used in scheduling and assigning space and in accounting for space for various purposes. In program budgeting, building and room data are essential for determining program costs and for establishing the facilities implications of proposed program changes. Current and accurate inventories are crucial for projecting future needs for facilities. The inventory makes meaningful comparisons with other institutions possible. At the state and federal planning levels, inventory information is useful for assessing facilities implications of proposed new program emphases, determining needs for maintenance and additions, and establishing funding priorities. The building inventory should contain at least the following information for each building: gross area, assignable area, estimated replacement cost, condition, year of construction, and ownership. Many institutions may desire to collect additional data. The inventory should also distinguish rooms on the basis of at least the following characteristics: room use, institutional organizational unit, area, number of student stations (where applicable), and institutional program classification. Again, data may be maintained on a variety of other room characteristics.

Although the vocabulary of facilities planning and management is not complex, a common understanding of several important terms is necessary for conducting an inventory of existing facilities and projecting space needs. The following definitions are taken from Romney (1974): A *building* is a roofed structure for permanent or temporary shelter of persons, animals, plants, or equipment; *gross area* is the sum of all floor areas of a building, based on exterior dimensions; *assignable area* is the sum of the areas that can be used in all rooms by building occupants to carry out their functions; *nonassignable area* is the sum of the circulation, custodial, mechanical, and structural areas of a building; *room use codes* identify the uses to which rooms are actually put (for example, classroom, class laboratory, office, greenhouse, or lounge); and *program classification codes* identify the institutional programs or activities carried out in particular rooms.

With respect to program classification codes, institutional programs are defined in the *Program Classification Structure* (Collier, 1978) to include instruction, research, public service, academic support, student services, institutional administration, physical plant operations, student financial support, and independent operations. Each program, in turn, is divided into a number of subprograms. (Each room will have both a room use code and a program classification code, and in general a space in any room use category may be assigned to any program classfication.)

The availability of a buildings and rooms inventory, when considered in conjunction with other institutional data, will enable an institution to compute various measures of its facilities use. Several of these indices are discussed below.

Space Use in General. Standards for using space are arbitrary; they tend to be based on normative practice, although in some cases they may be derived from theoretical computations (McConnell, Holy, and Semans, 1955, p. 9). Although they are normative, space factors can be very useful in determining how effectively a given college or university is using space, as compared to similar institutions.

Space factors vary from broad general measures, such as square feet of academic space per FTE student, to very detailed measures, such as square feet of assembly or food service space per student (State of New Jersey, 1970). The broad measures tend to be used most often for assessing the efficiency of facilities use by state systems or other aggregate groups of institutions. The extremely detailed standards are more often applied to planning new institutions or additional facilities at existing institutions. Broad measures, however, are useful in considering the efficiency of facilities use at a given institution. Granted that no two institutions are identical, if a given institution is significantly above or below the norm for space use at similar institutions, planners should carefully determine the reasons for this divergence.

The following sections describe some of the more commonly used standards for space utilization. In each case, illustrations from public and private institutions in North Carolina are used to show the range of institutional values, as measured against these standards (North Carolina State Commission on Higher Education Facilities, 1981).

Assignable Square Feet of Academic Space per FTE Student. Early U.S. Office of Education studies used 100 square feet of academic space per FTE student as a general planning standard for the universe of higher education institutions. *Academic space*, as used in this standard, includes, in broad terms, all the spaces on a campus except those used for museums and galleries, social and cultural development, student auxiliary services, intercollegiate athletics, faculty and staff services, public relations and development, and independent operations. Areas incapable of use are also excluded from this definition.

A subsequent Office of Education study developed the following more detailed normative values by level and control of institution (Norris, 1969):

	Total	*Public*	*Private*
University	136	132	150
Four-year	98	93	103
Two-year	70	70	75
All Institutions	107	103	115

The Norris report notes that these criteria were developed for an ad hoc federal assessment of facilities needs and suggests that they should not be used for other purposes. This author has found them useful, however, in making general assessments of the adequacy of current facilities and in projecting future needs.

Fall 1980 data for institutions in North Carolina are quite consistent with these standards. The public major research universities had an average of 126 assignable square feet of academic space per FTE student, compared to the criterion of 132. The entire universe of public and private higher education institutions in North Carolina had an average of 107, precisely meeting the standard. The average for the fifty-eight institutions in the public community college system was 82, compared to the standard of 70. It is interesting to note, however, that the institutional range was from 49 to 229 assignable square feet. This degree of variation illustrates at least two important considerations in facilities planning.

The first consideration is that new facilities are added as discrete buildings to support particular functions, rather than as increments of space to satisfy a formula. The average time that elapses from commitment of financing to occupancy of an academic building is around three years. Typically, the need for facilities becomes rather critical before a new building is funded, and normally the size of the new structure is based on a projection of needs over a considerable period of time. The result is that, in years of planned increased enrollments, this index tends to fall very low just before the new facilities come on line and to rise rather dramatically after they enter the inventory. This effect, of course, is most pronounced at smaller institutions, with their more limited inventory bases.

The second consideration is the impact that economy of scale has. In the case of institutions with comparable programs, the smaller institution requires somewhat more space per FTE student than that needed at the larger college. Where the North Carolina community college system is concerned, the institution with 229 assignable square feet per FTE student had only thirty FTE students, while the two largest institutions in the system had fifty-two and forty-nine students, respectively. Assignable square feet of academic space per FTE student, then, is a useful planning standard for systems or groups of institutions, but one that should be applied with some care and consideration of other factors in the case of a single institution.

Capacity/Enrollment Ratio. The capacity/enrollment ratio is the figure derived by dividing the total assignable square feet of instructional and library space by the total student contact hours of instruction per week. *Instructional and library space* consists of classrooms, class laboratories, special class laboratories, individual study laboratories, instructional faculty offices, and the service areas of all the above facilities, including libraries. In general terms, it is the sum of all the space directly used in the institution's instructional program.

The capacity/enrollment ratio was a major criterion for the objective priority ranking of applications under the federal Higher Education Facilities Act of 1963. The capacity/enrollment ratio measures the space available for the instructional program of the institution, as compared to the previous criterion, which considered space dedicated to all the academic programs of the institution.

We are not aware that any normative value has been established nationally for the capacity/enrollment ratio. Our experience suggests that ratios between 3.00 and 4.00 are in a desirable range. Applications below 3.00 tend to establish a high priority of need under the federal facilities program. As a norm, North Carolina uses a ratio of 4.00. The 1980 ratio for all North Carolina public and private institutions of higher education was 4.25. The community college system had a ratio of 3.06, the public senior institutions were very close to the statewide ratio of 4.00, and private institutions tended to exceed this figure. The capacity/enrollment ratio, then, is a useful measure for determining relative need for instructional and library facilities among institutions.

Average Weekly Hours of Instruction in Classrooms. Early facilities studies dealt largely with the scheduled use of classrooms and class laboratories (Halstead, 1974). One reason was the ease and attractiveness of analyzing scheduled spaces; another was the mistaken idea that college physical plants consisted largely of classrooms and class laboratories. Actually, these two categories of space account for about one-third of total facilities at the average institution. The percentage can vary from around 20 percent at major research universities to over 60 percent at some community colleges.

Despite this limitation, analysis of classroom use remains an important element in studies of space use. The most prevalent standard is that classrooms should be scheduled to be in use an average of 30 hours per week. Almost two decades of observation and experience suggest, however, that this standard is relatively difficult to attain, particularly at institutions that do not have major evening programs. For example, the average for all North Carolina institutions in 1980 was 21.8 hours per week. One of sixteen senior public institutions exceeded 30 hours per week, as did nine of fifty-eight community colleges and technical institutions. This standard is based on the facilities doctrine that classrooms should be available for institutionwide scheduling. In practice, of course, many classrooms are assigned to a particular instructional department or to an individual faculty member.

Average Weekly Hours of Instruction in Class Laboratories. The most common standard is that class laboratories should be scheduled 20 hours per week. Again, this standard is relatively difficult to achieve, especially at universities with complex and specialized graduate programs. The 1980 average for all institutions in North Carolina was 16.6 hours per week. The state community college system exceeded the standard, with an average of 22.6 hours. In contrast, the public universities averaged 11.2 hours, and the private institutions reported an average of 7.0 hours.

Classroom Space Factors. The preceding two standards consider only the number of hours per week a room is scheduled. Two other factors contribute to the efficiency with which a scheduled room is used — the number of square feet of space used per student station and the percentage of student stations occupied when the room is in use. The *space factor* is an index number, which incorporates these three aspects of room use.

As already noted, the general standard is that a classroom should be scheduled 30 hours per week; the most useful norm for a student station is 16 square feet. This figure is based on the typical classroom, with forty large armchair desks. The space needed per student station may vary from 9 square feet for an auditorium equipped with small armchair desks to 30 square feet for a seminar room equipped with tables and chairs. The general standard is that 60 percent of the student stations should be occupied when a classroom is in use.

The space factor, which is actually the assignable square feet of teaching space per student contact hour per week, is computed as follows:

$$\text{Space Factor} = \frac{\text{assignable square feet per station}}{\text{hours per week used} \times \text{percent station occupancy}}$$

Using the values above produces the following:

$$\text{Classroom Space Factor} = \frac{16}{30 \times 60\%} = 0.89$$

In 1980, the classroom space factor for all institutions of higher education in North Carolina was 1.29, which was above the standard, since a low figure reflects more intensive space use. The public research universities attained the standard of 0.89; the state range by institution was from a low of 0.65 to a high of 4.89.

Class Laboratory Space Factors. This measure is more difficult and less meaningful than the ones for classrooms, since the space required per student station in class laboratories varies widely by academic discipline. A class laboratory station for music requires from 15 to 20 square feet, while from 100 to 150 square feet are needed for automotive technologies, to cite two extremes of the distribution.

One useful approach to this measure is to divide class laboratories into two groups, academic and engineering/mechanical, with a student station norm of 40 square feet for the former and 100 square feet for the latter. The standard is for 80 percent of student stations to be occupied when the room is in use. The accompanying standard is that the laboratory be scheduled 20 hours per week.

Using the formula set out in the last section, we arrive at space factors of 2.50 for academic laboratories and 6.25 for engineering/mechanical laboratories. Obviously, because of the varying sizes of class laboratory student stations, this factor is more useful for illustrating the dynamics of laboratory use and comparing similar laboratories than for making broad interinstitutional comparisons.

How Are the Results of Facilities Analysis Used in Planning?

The results of facilities analysis are an essential element of the facilities planning cycle, which in turn is a component of the strategic planning process at the institution. Facilities planning also depends on other resource-analysis and program data (Dahnke and others, *Manual Six,* 1971).

Facilities constitute another of the resources of an institution of higher education (Kotler and Murphy, 1981). After analyzing its environment in terms of threats and opportunities, an institution should undertake an analysis of its resource position with respect to personnel, funds, facilities, and systems. The object is to build on the major strengths of the institution and avoid those areas where its resources are too weak. The inventory procedure already described will have provided this information about the institution's facilities.

The environment and resource analyses provide the information base for thinking about basic institutional objectives and goals. The first step in this process is a review of the mission or basic purpose of the institution. Starting from an accepted mission, the institution formulates goals. Goals are statements of major variables the institution will emphasize, such as student enrollment, alumni giving, and reputation. Goals, in turn, are broken down into objectives, which are specific as to magnitude, time, and responsibility. For example, the student recruitment and admissions office will be responsible for reaching an enrollment of 2,800 students, including 840 first-time freshmen in the fall of 1983.

The institution then undertakes a process of program definition and planning that involves strategy formulation, organization design, and systems design calculated to achieve the goals. One step in this process is to determine whether or not the facilities of the institution will be adequate to support its goals during the planning period. That process is outlined in the following section.

Facilities Projections. Only selected elements of the program planning data are necessary to support the facilities projection process. Elements of program planning particularly necessary for facilities planning include projections of (1) instructional loads, (2) faculty and support staff in the academic departments, (3) support employees in nonacademic departments, and (4) numbers of students and others to be served in auxiliary enterprise facilities (residential, dining, student health, recreation, and so on).

The facilities manuals (Dahnke and others, 1971) contain detailed procedures for translating these workloads into facilities requirements. Normative standards are cited for each type of space. A detailed procedure is set out for individual institutions, and a more generalized procedure is outlined for systems of higher education. In this manner, the facilities needed to house the projected programs of an institution at some time in the future are determined. This requirement is then compared with the existing space inventory, including any facilities that have been funded and will be on line by the data for which planning is being done. This comparison may show an excess of facilities, an approximate balance, a deficit in facilities, or the need to reprogram existing facilities to meet changing requirements.

Time lags and the uneven flow of facilities planning should be noted. Institutions rarely if ever find it feasible to add one classroom, one class laboratory, or one faculty office to meet a current or near-term need. The typical pattern is that enrollment increases or other program growth create pressures on the total facilities inventory of the institution. The institution then determines the type of building that will alleviate these pressures most effectively. That building is normally designed with excess capacity to meet projected needs in that program area over a period of years. Obtaining financing for a new facility at either a public or a private institution of higher education often takes two or more years. The average time that elapses from commitment of financing to occupancy is around three years. These characteristics of the process highlight the need to project and plan facilities as far in the future as the required data bases will allow.

Some Practical Applications. The procedures outlined in this chapter incorporate a great deal of precise mathematical detail. It should be emphasized, however, that the issues to be decided upon are often presented to planners in much grosser terms, especially when planning is being done at the state system level. For example, if a four-year institution has only 70 square feet of academic space per FTE student and enrollments are projected to increase modestly, the institution will need to plan additional facilities to accommodate existing and projected enrollments. If a similar institution has 140 square feet of academic space per FTE student, then additional specialized academic facilities will have to be justified on the basis of the new or expanding requirements of a particular academic program. In the latter case, a consideration of the possible conversion or reprogramming of underused facilities might be indicated. If classrooms are used only fifteen or twenty hours per week, justifying a new classroom building would be difficult. In the same manner, if science class laboratories are used eight hours a week and each member of the related faculties has a private office, then the need for a new science building is also questionable.

Over a decade ago, the president of a college came to my office to discuss a substantial proposed building program at his institution. His college had recently completed a new library and a new science building and was facing a trend of seriously declining enrollments. We compared his space inventory with that of similar institutions in the state. At the end of this process, he concluded that his college could accommodate between two and three times the current enrollment in the existing plant.

Decline in the numbers of traditional eighteen- to twenty-four-year-old students, a group that now represents about 80 percent of the college instructional load (Bareither, 1981), coupled with increasing competition from other educational delivery systems, does suggest that the demand for traditional education in traditional schools will also decline at a fairly rapid rate. This trend will give rise to excess space at some institutions and will accelerate the need to redesign existing space to meet the changing program requirements.

The foregoing examples may seem extreme, but they illustrate types of issues that confront boards of trustees, state higher education agencies, and state legislatures on a continuing basis. On the one hand, these examples suggest that utilization data can narrow the parameters of decision making. On the other hand, no two institutions of higher education are identical; ultimately, decisions regarding new facilities must be made in the context of the mission, goals, and objectives of a given institution.

Additional Steps in Facilities Planning. This chapter has described the procedures by which institutional researchers can analyze facilities resources and project facilities needs. Facilities planning involves at least six additional steps, which will only be mentioned here, since they generally are not the responsibility of institutional research personnel. A brief description of each of these steps appears in the facilities manuals (Dahnke and others, *Manual One,* 1971).

1. The *facilities development program* is the result of the process by which the projected additional space requirements are aggregated into identifiable building units.
2. *Site planning* is the process by which the map of the campus is revised to indicate the disappearance of any buildings that are to be demolished and to show the appearance of new buildings, other physical facilities, and landscaping.
3. The *capital development program* specifies building projects to be undertaken, lists them in priority order, and projects estimated costs.

4. *Building programming* involves specifying the activities to be housed in the building, the amounts of each type of space to be provided, basic design requirements, utility and equipment requirements, preliminary cost estimates, and a timetable.
5. *Design development* is the process by which general requirements for the building, as expressed in the building program, are translated into detailed construction drawings and specifications.
6. *Space management* is the process by which existing facilities are allocated to current programs or organizational units.

Conclusion

Facilities analysis is the examination of a higher education complex and its buildings and of their relationship to the present and future ability of the institution to perform its mission. The process is important because facilities are an essential and costly resource of institutions. The first step in facilities analysis is the completion of a building and room inventory. A number of normative standards are available to assess the efficiency with which facilities are being used. The inventory information should be considered along with data on instructional loads, staffing, and levels of auxiliary services. These same programmatic measures, when expressed as future goals in the strategic planning process, can be used to project future facilities requirements. Facilities planning, then, is an interactive part of the strategic planning process of an institution. It is essential to have data on the volume of institutional program activity, so that the facilities plan may become a part of the institution's strategic planning.

References

Bareither, H. D. "Space Management and Projection." In D. K. Halstead (Ed.), *Higher Education: A Bibliographic Handbook.* Vol. 2. Washington, D.C.: The National Institute of Education, 1981.
Bareither, H. D., and Schillinger, J. L. *University Space Planning.* Urbana: University of Illinois Press, 1968.
Collier, D. J. *Program Classification Structure.* (2nd ed.) Boulder, Colo.: National Center for Higher Education Management Systems, 1978.
Dahnke, H. L., Jones, D. P., Mason, T. R., and Romney, L. C. *Higher Education Facilities Planning and Management Manuals.* Boulder, Colo.: National Center for Higher Education Management Systems, 1971.
Halstead, D. K. *Statewide Planning in Higher Education.* Washington, D.C.: U.S. Government Printing Office, 1974.
Kotler, P., and Murphy, P. E. "Strategic Planning for Higher Education." *Journal of Higher Education,* 1981, *52* (5), 470–489.
McConnell, T. R., Holy, T. C., and Semans, H. H. *A Restudy of the Needs of California in Higher Education.* Sacramento: California State Department of Education, 1955.
Norris, C. G. *Federal Support for Higher Education Construction: Current Programs and Future Needs.* Washington, D.C.: U.S. Office of Education, 1969.

North Carolina State Commission on Higher Education Facilities. *Facilities Inventory and Utilization Study*. Raleigh: North Carolina State Commission on Higher Education Facilities, 1981.

Osso, T. (Ed.). *Higher Education Facilities Classification and Inventory Procedures Manual*. Washington, D.C.: National Center for Educational Statistics, 1968.

Romney, L. C. *Facilities Inventory and Classification Manual, 1973*. Washington, D.C.: U.S. Office of Education, 1974.

Russell, J. D., and Doi, J. I. *Manual for Studies of Space Utilization in Colleges and Universities*. Athens, Ohio: American Association of Collegiate Registrars and Admissions Officers, 1957.

State of New Jersey Department of Higher Education. *Facilities Standards and Planning Manual for New Jersey County Community Colleges*. Trenton, N.J.: Department of Higher Education, 1970.

Wheeler, C. L. *Facilities Inventory and Utilization Study, Fall of 1967*. Raleigh: North Carolina State Commission on Higher Education Facilities, 1969.

Charles L. Wheeler is currently assistant vice-president for research and public service of the University of North Carolina and director of the North Carolina State Commission on Higher Education Facilities. He has served previously as assistant vice-president for planning of the University of North Carolina, special assistant to the governor of North Carolina, director of legislative research in Kentucky, and assistant state welfare director in North Carolina.

Progress toward achieving university goals can be assessed by using existing records, special data-collection efforts, and special studies.

Assessing Institutional Goals

Linda K. Pratt
Donald R. Reichard

An institution's missions, goals, and objectives are all involved in assessing institutional goals. The mission is a statement of educational philosophy, which may include a description of special populations to be served. It changes infrequently and provides a long-term sense of identity to an institution. Goals, in contrast, provide a sense of direction for the shorter term. An institution may have several goals that guide its activity and efforts for periods of two or more years. Objectives are much more specific statements, which describe activities and related outcomes for short periods of time, usually one year or less.

Fenske (1980) presents a definition of goals that reflects the broad consensus of many other authors. He defines goals as statements of university purpose that fall between extremely broad statements, such as those contained in the institutional mission, and specific descriptions of various operations within a university. For example, one element in the mission of a women's college might be to educate young women to meet the challenges of life. A related goal would be to prepare young women to compete with men for jobs and honors in all phases of life. A specific objective related to this mission–goal pairing would be to have 50 percent of the graduating class admitted to highly selective graduate schools or universities.

In another area, one aspect of the mission of a traditionally black college might be to prepare all its students to enter the mainstream of American society. A related goal might be to provide opportunities for students to pre-

N. P. Uhl (Ed.). *Using Research for Strategic Planning.* New Directions for
Institutional Research, no. 37. San Francisco: Jossey-Bass, March 1983.

pare for specific careers such as accounting, engineering, or nursing. Specific objectives might be to find jobs in the major field for 90 percent of all business majors within three months of their graduation or to increase the rate of nursing students passing the state licensing examination from 70 percent to 95 percent. Obviously, a broad mission statement can generate several goals, and each goal, in turn, can create many objectives.

Goals such as those stated here, as well as those included in anthologies like the *Institutional Goals Inventory* (*IGI*) (Educational Testing Service, 1972), imply a desired outcome. A key element is the translation of broad goals, which may prove difficult to measure, into more specific and measurable objectives. The National Center for Higher Education Management Systems (NCHEMS) has published a manual (Micek, Service, and Lee, 1975) that contains an extensive list of institutional outcome variables, each paired with several potential measures. The task of the college or university, then, is to translate the implied outcomes of goals into outcome variables and, finally, to identify specific measures. Uhl (1978) describes a procedure for achieving this translation, which involves broad-based university committees. Table 1 gives an example of a goal, an appropriate outcome variable for that goal, and several potential measures. The outcome variable, in effect, defines the outcome implied in the goals. The outcome measures represent alternative strategies for measuring the outcome variable.

The goal, the outcome variable, and one or more of the outcome measures can be combined in various ways to develop specific objectives. As can be seen from the example in Table 1, the goal provides the target population for the objective (the students), while the outcome measure defines the measurement tool. All that is needed to develop a complete objective is a date for achievement and a criterion appropriate to the outcome measure. A complete objective might be: "The average student's score on those items from tests that measure depth of knowledge in special fields of study will increase by 15 percent (the criterion level) by 1985."

The specific objective developed from a single goal statement will vary with the unit developing the objectives. Thus, each department or administrative unit within a college or a university may have a different objective related to the same overall institutional goal.

Obviously, goals are the cornerstone of effective planning, and yet there are those who question the need for goals. As Fenske indicates, "The question 'Why study goals?' is somewhat annoying to most planners and researchers, in that the answer seems so obvious, even axiomatic. One of the few things organizational theorists agree on is the necessity of defining and studying goals" (Fenske, 1980, p. 178).

If goals are defined as statements of desired institutional direction, they must exist if planning is to occur. Nevertheless, many institutions seem to function, plan, and move forward in the absence of clearly defined goals. If goals are central to planning and planning is necessary for development, how can this situation occur?

Table 1. An Example of the Relationship of a Goal to Outcome Variables and Specific Measurements

Goal	Outcome Variables[b]	Potential Measures[b]
To help students acquire depth of knowledge in at least one academic discipline.[a]	1.1.1.02 *Specialized Knowledge* The familiarity with and understanding of facts and principles in the particular fields in which the student elects to study. The student's depth of knowledge.	1.1.1.02 *Specialized Knowledge Measures* Average student score on those items from tests (CLEP Subject Exams or GRE Area Exams) that measure depth of knowledge in special fields of study. Average student change in depth of knowledge by discipline area, as determined by comparing entering specialized knowledge test scores to subsequent test scores (on CLEP Subject Exams or GRE Area Exams) after _____ years. Number of graduates accepting emloyment in major field of study as a percentage of total graduates in that field. Number of students passing certification or licensing exams (bar exam, CPA) on first attempt as a percentage of all students taking the exam. Average student-reported score on scale measuring the degree of satisfaction with knowledge gained in specialized fields of study (based on a student survey). Number of graduates accepted for study in postbaccalaureate degree programs as a percentage of those applying.

[a]*Source:* Educational Testing Service, 1972.
[b]*Source:* Micek, Service, and Lee, 1975, p. 257.

There are two possible answers to this apparent contradiction. First, the mission and the related objectives of some institutions may be either so well defined or so much a part of the cultural milieu of the institution that formal statement is not necessary. This may be the case if all those involved in the institution (the faculty, students, the staff, administrators, alumni, and trustees) share a common purpose or purposes. Second, an institution may develop and grow in the absence of goals when a strong, charismatic leader guides and directs the institution. In this case, the goals exist, not on paper or in the culture of the institution, but in the mind of a single person. The danger is that the institution may flounder, directionless, if this leader leaves. The situation is not always so straightforward. Most often, goals are neither universally shared by all constituent groups in an institution nor clearly defined by the leadership of a single individual. Most institutions must use some process to identify or select goals, which then form a "road map" for the institution, defining what the institution wants to achieve.

One note of caution should be injected: When there is less than perfect agreement, there is a temptation to list many goals in an attempt to satisfy everyone. This temptation should be avoided. If goals are to provide a focus for institutional plans, the number of the goals must be limited; otherwise, attention and resources will be spread so thin that no single goal will be achieved.

Selection of Goals

After an institution reaches the conclusion that some formal process must be used to identify goals, other decisions must be made. Should an institution use a collection of goal statements developed by an outside person or group, or should a list be developed expressly for the institution? Which constituent groups should be involved in the process, and how many persons from each group? Which process or processes should be used to select a defined set of goals? Who is responsible for coordination of the process?

Several compilations of goal statements are available to institutions that do not wish to write their own goals. The best-known and one of the most extensive is the *IGI*. There are now three versions of this instrument—the original version, suitable for public and larger private four-year colleges and universities; and two newer versions, the *Small College Goals Inventory* and the *Community College Goals Inventory* (see the "Additional Resources" section at the end of this chapter for further information). The *IGI* has ninety items, with room for the institution to add twenty more. The Educational Testing Service has published guides for use of the *IGI,* which describe the instrument, suggest appropriate methods for conducting a goals study (Peterson and Uhl, 1975), and provide comparative data (Peterson and Uhl, 1977).

Regardless of the method chosen to develop a pool of goal statements, once that pool is developed, some method must be devised to select a subset for use in planning, since there will almost certainly be more goals than any one institution can address in a reasonable period of time.

There are, of course, several methods for selecting high-priority goals. One of the simplest, from an administrative point of view, is the survey. If this approach is adopted, a large set of goal statements is generally sent to individuals chosen from each institutional constituent group. The results of the survey are compiled, and the highest-ranked (or highest-rated) goals become the current goals of the institution.

Many goal inventories, notably the *IGI,* ask participants to rate goals in two ways. First, the participant is asked to rate the goal as to its current importance, the *Is* response; and, second, the participant rates the goal as to the importance it should have in the future, the *Should Be* response. In selecting goals for attention, it is especially important to consider the goals that have the highest *Should Be* ratings, accompanied by a large discrepancy between the *Is* and *Should Be* ratings. These are the areas that represent potential problems.

The survey approach has the advantage of being relatively inexpensive, requiring a minimum of each participant's time and allowing inclusion of a greater number of participants. In fact, the entire population of some constituent groups (such as trustees, administrators, and, perhaps, the faculty) can often be included. Care should be taken, however, to compose a clear and persuasive cover letter; otherwise, response rates may be lower than desired. This letter probably should be signed by the president or by the chairman of the board of trustees. One drawback to the survey method is the fact that the survey does not provide a means of resolving conflicts among the various constituent groups. If there is substantial disagreement, the difference must be resolved by the person who compiles the results. This solution probably will not be completely satisfactory to any of the groups.

A second technique for conflict resolution, which maintains many of the advantages of the survey approach, is the Delphi technique. The Delphi technique was developed in the 1950s by the RAND Corporation as a means of resolving conflicting assumptions among military personnel and advisers about defense problems. A modified form of this technique, suitable for a goals study, could involve mailing the goals survey to samples of institutional constituents, summarizing the results, and sending the results back to the same sample for re-evaluation. Participants would have the opportunity to justify their responses, and some or all of these written justifications would be returned along with the results. After two or more rounds, the responses should converge, yielding a set of goals acceptable to the various constituent groups. Uhl (1971) describes such a study performed at five quite diverse postsecondary institutions. Chapter Eight describes in detail this use of the Delphi technique.

The advantages of conducting a Delphi study using the survey technique are similar to those of using a survey. In addition, conflict among constituent groups should be reduced, since convergence of opinion almost always occurs. The return rate can become a problem, however, if participants do not view this task as important.

The survey and Delphi methods are sound, practical, and relatively inexpensive ways of assessing institutional goals, but sometimes face-to-face interaction among participants is necessary. There are other procedures combining one or more elements of the survey and Delphi methods and involving this type of interaction. One, the group Delphi goals technique, was developed by the National Laboratory for Higher Education (Pratt, 1973) and field tested at several sites. The basic process is the Delphi technique. All participants rate goals and justify their responses. The responses are summarized, and the process is repeated. After two or three repetitions, a defined subset of goals tends to emerge. Then, all participants meet to complete the process on a single day, so that almost all complete the entire process. The number of participants using this procedure is strictly limited, however, while broad participation in the goal-setting process is often desirable. The logistical problems are complex, but the manual describing the process addressed most of these. (See the "Additional Resources" section at the end of this chapter for information on obtaining this manual.) The group Delphi goals technique does not encourage discussion of the goals, although informal conversations among participants will occur.

A second group Delphi technique was developed by Baker (1972) (see "Additional Resources"). This process was developed for junior and community colleges and involved a Delphi-like procedure. Teams of four persons, one from each of four constituent groups, discuss the goals and reach a consensus. Open discussions of the goals take place within each team, and team responses and justifications are summarized and returned for the second and subsequent rounds. The number of participants is much greater than in the group method described previously. Up to 100 persons can participate. Discussion within teams is encouraged and tends to be lively. The logistics are complex enough so that a facilitator thoroughly familiar with the process probably should be present to coordinate it. The four processes described here for selecting institutional goals are only a sample of the possible methods; each institution should adopt a method based on its own needs. For example, Uhl (1978) described a method in which Delphi results from a survey were combined with committee procedures.

The goal-setting procedure is generally best coordinated by the office of institutional research. Assuming that university planning is not a function of this office, the planning officer and all the major administrators should be involved in making the initial decision to conduct the study and also should be consulted in selecting a format. As part of this process, institutional research office personnel may want to suggest a goal-identification procedure, outlining its advantages and disadvantages. The institutional research office can distribute instruments and collect data in the survey type of study, but, as indicated earlier, the president or the chairman of the board of trustees should sign the initial introductory letter. Several chief administrative personnel should take active roles in the process, although the office of institutional research may make all the arrangements, and the institutional researcher or an outside consultant may act as facilitator.

Examples of Goal Assessment

Many institutions develop institutional goals, but few continue to the next step in the process—assessing the extent to which the institution has achieved its goals. The remainder of this chapter will be devoted to exploring some methods for assessing progress toward achieving goals. Many examples will contain a single evaluation strategy and thus employ only one measure. These examples are intended to illustrate a variety of approaches to goal assessment. It should be emphasized, however, that an institution probably will want to employ more than one strategy (and, hence, more than one measure) when assessing progress toward meeting goals.

The examples will be divided into three frequently encountered categories—examples illustrating the use of existing institutional records, examples illustrating assessments that require special reports or analytical studies, and examples employing measures of constituent attitudes and perceptions. The institutional research office, because of its expertise, should coordinate these collection efforts.

Use of Existing Records. One goal that can be used to illustrate assessment through existing or regularly maintained institutional records is that of broadening a scholarship program designed to attract students with high academic potential but without concern for financial need. The most direct method of assessing progress toward this goal is to determine the number of academic (as opposed to need-based, athletic, or minority-presence) scholarships offered to students. Additional measures could be the average amount of the scholarships and the total amount of money devoted to academic scholarships. Note, as with many of the examples that will follow, the importance of collecting baseline data. Progress must have a referent. For this particular goal, the baseline data would be the number of scholarships offered in the years prior to the time when this goal was given special attention, the amount of academic scholarship money distributed, and the average size of the scholarships. An increase in any or all of these related measures could be interpreted as progress toward achieving the goal. Whether or not this progress is satisfactory can be determined only with criteria set by the institution.

A second goal that could be assessed by examination of institutional records is that of rewarding excellence in research and scholarly inquiry. If the institution has a faculty evaluation system, it also should have some record of the scholarly and creative activities of each faculty member, as well as a record of the faculty members who receive promotion, tenure, and/or merit pay increments each year. By examining these records, the institution can determine if those faculty members who engaged in scholarly activities and received high performance ratings were given greater salary increases than their colleagues and were promoted at a faster rate. If records for the year prior to this goal's adoption are used as a base, in subsequent years there should be a clear increase in the scholarly and professional activities and in the salaries of those faculty members who emphasize these activities.

A third example of using university records to assess goal achievement could be assessment of a goal to improve campus security. Records of the activity of the security division, including the number and type of infractions reported, provide a good measure of the adequacy of campus security.

These examples represent three diverse goals that can be assessed by using the university records. There are several advantages to this approach: Base data are available in most cases, there is little if any disruption of institutional activities, this type of measure is unobtrusive and probably is not affected by the measurement itself, and the cost of collecting the data is minimal.

Special Reports and Analytical Studies. While existing records are often good measures of goal attainment, they are not always appropriate or available. Occasionally, an administrative office may need to make a special data-collection effort and compile these data into a special report. For example, if improving the image of the university in the local community is a goal, then the public relations office can be asked to prepare an annual report on efforts made to reach this goal. This report would probably specify efforts of the public relations office and include such items as copies of newspaper reports and a log of radio and television announcements.

Given a goal of encouraging faculty members to perform additional research, an institution could require each department to complete a special annual report. Data to be reported could include the number of research-oriented grant proposals submitted each year, the number and type of faculty research projects currently in progress, and the number of books and research articles published or presented by faculty members during the year.

Note that each of these examples involves using data that are readily available to the unit making the report, but which might not be collected or compiled if the report were not needed to assess the goal. Some institutional effort is required for this type of goal assessment, but the effort can be minimized with careful planning. For example, creating a set of newspaper articles and a log of radio and television announcements is relatively simple on a day-to-day basis. Creating the same log at the end of the year would be time consuming or even impossible. If special reports are needed, the units making them should be given detailed specifications as early as possible.

Often, simple tabular analysis of data is insufficient. If, for example, one goal of an institution were to reduce the discrepancy between the salaries of women faculty members and their male colleagues, analysis of covariance or multiple-regression analysis would be more effective and useful because it would allow statistical control of such variables as field and length of service.

Assessment Measuring Attitudes and Perceptions. A third method of assessing goals is by using instruments that measure the attitudes and perceptions of members of various constituent groups within the institution. The following examples describe several instruments that could be used to assess progress toward institutional goals. Other instruments are available. Institutions also may want to develop their own instruments or add special questions to some of those described here.

A goal shared by many colleges and universities is providing the background and specialization necessary for additional education in some professional, scientific, or scholarly field. Assessing progress in attaining this goal may take place at several times and may be made easier by the use of items for which normative data provide a basis of comparing the results. Thus, for example, similarly phrased questions from Pace's *Higher Education Measurement and Evaluation Kit* (1975) (see "Additional Resources") may be posed to entering students, who may be asked to state the extent to which they value a goal or possess a requisite skill or ability. If appropriate safeguards of validity are built into the research design, subsequent posing of the questions to the same students as upperclassmen or recent graduates may indicate progress toward attaining the desired goal. Similarly, assessing goal attainment may be approached by posing the same questions cross-sectionally to students in freshman through senior classes, as well as to recent graduates.

The sample cross-sectional data in Table 2 illustrate consistent increases in the percentages of freshmen, sophomores, juniors, and seniors who indicated that they benefited "very much" or "quite a bit" from obtaining background and specialization for advanced education in some professional, scientific, or scholarly field. Differences by class may be explained in part by selective retention of students. In assessing perceived benefits for a particular item, interpretive power may be gained by comparing the relative rankings of importance attached to the related items in Table 2. Patterns of perceived benefits should be emphasized, rather than findings from a single administration of an item in isolation from other items.

When longitudinal data are not available, discrepancy analyses incorporating a series of actual (*Is*) versus ideal (*Should Be*) comparisons also may be helpful in assessing differences between expectations and outcomes. In this regard, differences between the ideal and the actual attainment of specific goals may be evaluated. If a survey indicates that 80 percent of respondents value an outcome, but only 40 percent achieve that outcome, then the survey has identified an area in which stated goal criteria are not being met. Interpretive strength is also increased by comparing the responses of various subgroups — males and females, blacks and whites, or different majors in particular schools. Use of similarly phrased items will provide a basis for interinstitutional comparisons and/or comparisons with national normative data.

Studies related to perceptions of the possession or the enhancement of particular skills or abilities also can be helpful in assessing the attainment of educational goals or benefits and may have implications for departmental or general curricular reform. If an institution seeks to develop computer literacy

Table 2. Percentage of Students Who Report Progress or Who Have Benefitted "Very Much" or "Quite a Bit" by Race, Sex, and Class

	Total %	Race Black %	White %	Sex M %	F %	Fresh. %	Soph. %	Jr. %	Sr. %	Spec. Adult %
Vocational Benefits										
Background and specialization for further education in some professional scientific or scholarly field	65	58	67	73	64	42***	66	75	80	61
Bases for improved social and economic status	55	54	57	65*	53	39***	52	57	73	61
Vocabulary, terminology, and facts in various fields of knowledge	76	80***	60	80	74	63***	77	80	84	81
Vocational training—skills and techniques directly applicable to a job	44	41	45	46	44	27***	45	50	53	44
Humanistic Benefits										
Awareness of different philosophies, cultures, ways of life	65	55*	68	58	67	54	69	68	70	60
Broadened literary acquaintance and appreciation	53	45*	55	55	52	45*	49	56	59	66
Aesthetic sensitivity—appreciation and enjoyment of art, music and drama	53	39***	57	56	52	49	53	57	51	60
Writing and speaking—clear, correct, effective communication	49	47	50	56	47	45	46	44	59	50

*p < .05
**p < .01
***p < .001

for its graduates, then should it be concerned if only 5 percent of its graduates indicate that they possess the ability to use computers and analyze computer printouts. If campuswide computing resources are enhanced, what percentage of graduates should possess computer skills within the next three, five, or ten years? Similarly, if cooperating with a work team is regarded as an important attribute in the business community, then a school of business may need to examine its curricular offerings if fewer business graduates than graduates in other schools indicate that their studies have enhanced this attribute. Such findings need at least to be considered in developing discussions among persons involved in institutional or departmental planning and goal-setting processes.

The frequently cited goal of encouraging close relationships between the faculty and students may be assessed in part by items from the Professor's Scale, which is included in Pace (1975). Here, as with the Educational Benefits Scales (Pace, 1975), the examination of responses to individual items or to the entire scale by criteria of race, sex, or class may be helpful in interpreting longitudinal or cross-sectional data. Another interpretive dimension that may have great value is the use of interinsitutional data to compare findings from institutions of various types. In assessing faculty–student relationships, it may be helpful to know that fewer blacks than whites in predominantly white institutions believe this statement: "The professors go out of their way to help you." A similar finding in a predominantly black college could yield additional interpretive significance by suggesting that black students in general perceive some social distance between themselves and the faculty, regardless of whether the faculty is predominantly black or white. This could suggest in turn that the broad topic of faculty–student interaction needs more attention, both on predominantly white and predominantly black campuses.

This discussion has focused until now on instruments and goals related to students' perceptions and attitudes. There are also instruments suited for use with other constituent groups. The *Institutional Functioning Inventory* (*IFI*) (Educational Testing Service, 1970) is one such instrument. The *IFI* has scales composed of twelve items, each of which addresses some aspect of the climate of a college or a university. For example, one university had a goal of developing and maintaining a planning and budgeting process to ensure accountability, efficiency, and effectiveness in implementing goals and objectives. The Self-Study and Planning Scale of the *IFI* measures "the importance college leaders attach to continuous long-range planning for the total institution and to institutional research needed in formulating and revising plans" (ETS, 1970). The university was a participant in a long-range research project involving the *IFI* and, as part of that project, had given the *IFI* to the full-time instructional faculty in 1970. In 1976, the university undertook a planning project culminating in a nontraditional self-study for the Southern Association of Colleges and Schools. One objective of the process was to make all members of the university community aware of the planning effort and to involve as many persons as possible. When the *IFI* was given to a sample of faculty members in 1981, the results of this study effort were apparent. The mean response on the scale rose from 6.87 ($N = 157$, $SD = 2.92$) to 7.71 ($N = 51$, $SD = 2.68$). On certain items, such as "There is a long-range plan for the institution published for collegewide distribution," agreement rose from 32 percent in 1970 to 84 percent in 1981. This scale and several of the specific items on it seem to reflect progress toward achieving the goal. Although these data are not the only means of assessing progress toward this specific goal, they certainly represent one measure to be considered.

Notes on the Use of Data

Since goal attainment cannot be evaluated in a vacuum, it is important to use some sort of base data. Several means of establishing a base are given below:

1. The most straightforward method of establishing a base for comparison is determining the measure to be used and making the measurements before attempting to implement the goal.

2. If possible, measurements at intermediate points should be made. Trends can be established and fed back into the planning process. Resulting adjustments may then be made before the deadline established for achieving the goal.

3. If, for example, base data are not available for the senior class, then cross-sectional analysis comparing the freshman and senior classes in a single year can be useful. Since longitudinal data can be influenced by cultural events, and since the cross-sectional approach contains the inherent danger of comparing different groups, the use of both techniques is always best, whenever possible.

4. Some goal instruments, notably the *IGI,* ask for both *Is* and *Should Be* ratings. The ranking of the *Should Be* category identifies the important goals. When combined with the discrepancy between *Is* and *Should Be* categories, it helps identify the goals that should receive special attention. Reduction of the discrepancy can become a future measure of goal attainment.

The assessment of goals is a complex process. The role the office of institutional research should play in this process may extend well beyond the actual implementation of a goals study. As a resource agent, the office of institutional research may be able to identify other instruments that can be used, as well as other institutions whose prior experiences may warn of pitfalls. If the institutional research office has conducted prior studies indicating that certain outcomes are appropriate measures for demonstrating goal achievement among faculty members, students, administrators, or trustees, then the impact of these studies may be increased significantly.

There are no hard and fast rules for assessing goals; there are only general guidelines. Specifying the relationship between a goal and a set of outcomes by formulating clear objectives is the key to the process. Once this specification is made, the ingenuity of evaluators, the quality of institutional records, and the cooperation of departments in collecting base data will all provide the means for completing the process successfully.

Additional Sources

The *Small Colleges Goals Inventory* (*SCGI*) and the *Community Colleges Goals Inventory* (*CCGI*) are adaptations of the *Institutional Goals Inventory* (*IGI*). All three are identical in format. The *SCGI* is concerned with the priorities and goals of small liberal arts colleges. The *CCGI* speaks to the goals and constituencies of the typical community college. More information about the *SCGI* and the *CCGI* is available from Nancy Beck, ETS College and University Programs, Princeton, NJ 08541.

The manual describing the group Delphi technique can be obtained by writing to Dr. Linda K. Pratt at the Office of Research, Evaluation, and Planning, North Carolina Central University, Durham, NC 27707.

For more information concerning the group Delphi technique developed for use in junior and community colleges, write to Dr. George Baker, Professor of Education, Program in Community College Education, 348 Education Building, The University of Texas, Austin, TX 78712.

The *Higher Education Measurement and Evaluation Kit* (Pace, 1975) uses a number of loose-leaf minitests consisting of from five to fifteen items each, all related to a common theme or factor. Pace has also incorporated a set of additional measures into his *College Student Experiences* questionnaire (1979). For more information, write to C. Robert Pace and Associates, Laboratory for Research on Higher Education, Graduate School of Education, University of California, Los Angeles, CA 90024.

References

Baker, G., III. *Goal Setting for Organizational Accountability: A Leadership Strategy (GOALS)*. Durham, N.C.: National Laboratory for Higher Education, 1972.

Educational Testing Service. *Institutional Functioning Inventory*. (Rev. ed.) Princeton, N.J.: Educational Testing Service, 1970.

Educational Testing Service. *Institutional Goals Inventory*. Princeton, N.J.: Educational Testing Service, 1972.

Fenske, R. H. "Setting Institutional Goals and Objectives." In P. Jedamus, M. Peterson, and Associates (Eds.), *Improving Academic Management*. San Francisco: Jossey-Bass, 1980.

Micek, S. S., Service, A. L., and Lee, Y. S. *Outcome Measures and Procedures Manual: Field Review Edition*. Technical Report No. 70. Boulder, Colo.: National Center for Higher Education Management Systems, 1975.

Pace, C. R., and Associates. *Higher Education Measurement and Evaluation Kit.* Los Angeles: UCLA Laboratory for Research on Higher Education, 1975.

Peterson, R. E., and Uhl, N. P. *IGI Comparative Data.* Princeton, N.J.: Educational Testing Service, 1975.

Peterson, R. E., and Uhl, N. P. *Formulating College and University Goals: A Guide for Using the IGI.* Princeton, N.J.: Educational Testing Service, 1977.

Pratt, L. K. *Administrative Manual for Group Delphi Goals Technique.* Durham, N.C.: National Laboratory for Higher Education, 1973.

Uhl, N. P. *Identifying Institutional Goals.* Durham, N.C.: National Laboratory for Higher Education, 1971. (ERIC/ED 049713)

Uhl, N. P. "A Case Study of Goals-Oriented Research." In R. H. Fenske (Ed.), *New Directions for Institutional Research: Using Goals in Research and Planning,* no. 19. San Francisco: Jossey-Bass, 1978.

Linda K. Pratt is director of the Office of Research, Evaluation, and Planning and professor of psychology at North Carolina Central University in Durham. Previously, she was coordinator of evaluation and a research associate at the National Laboratory for Higher Education, also in Durham. She received her Ph.D. in experimental psychology from Texas Christian University.

Donald R. Reichard is director of the Office of Institutional Research and adjunct associate professor of higher education at the University of North Carolina at Greensboro. Previously, he was a research associate with the Southern Regional Educational Board in Atlanta, Georgia. He received his Ph.D. in higher education from Michigan State University.

*Timeliness, creativity, and effective communication are necessary
in institutional research before it can be channeled into the mainstream of
collegial decision making, policy formulation, and planning.*

Institutional Fact Book:
Catalyst for an Integrated
Institutional Research Program

Glynton Smith

Broad understanding of an institution is fundamental to strategic planning.
Information and communication are integral parts of this understanding. Information entails a "creative intervention of human intelligence in the organization and aggregation of data and an intent to communicate" (Arns, 1979).
There are many ways to serve basic information needs and to communicate
the results of institutional research. One practical way of combining these
aims is an institutional fact book.

A recent National Center for Higher Education Management Systems
(NCHEMS) survey reported priorities of college presidents regarding potential planning and management improvements at their institutions (Patrick and
Caruthers, 1980). These survey results have implications for institutional researchers. Most public college and university presidents did not perceive a

Appreciation is expressed to Dr. Joe B. Ezell, associate vice-president for institutional planning, Georgia State University, and to Dr. David M. Morgan, staff director of the Governor's Committee on Postsecondary Education in Georgia, both wise
planning specialists. I also acknowledge the influence of my friend and former boss,
Mr. Shealy McCoy, treasurer of the Georgia Board of Regents and vice-chancellor for
fiscal affairs of the University System of Georgia.

N. P. Uhl (Ed.). *Using Research for Strategic Planning.* New Directions for
Institutional Research, no. 37. San Francisco: Jossey-Bass, March 1983.

need for additional data reports, the mainstay of many institutional research offices. Their area of highest priority was communicating institutional strengths to general audiences (students, parents, the faculty, the staff, trustees, and the public) and to state-level audiences (the budget office and the legislature).

Standards for communicating the results of institutional research have been suggested (Fincher, 1979). Presentations at Association for Institutional Research (AIR) forums provide little indication that the membership has taken these standards seriously. Moreover, a panel of AIR past presidents warned that too much faith is placed in fashionable models and techniques that hide rather than illuminate the mosaic of institutions; institutional researchers were criticized for providing "datamation" instead of information. This panel raised the question of whether or not institutional researchers are number-driven, unthinking middlemen between the computer and the policy makers (Past Presidents' Panel, 1979, p. 36).

Widely shareable information is needed as background on issues facing institutions. Typically, decision making, policy formulation, and planning in public colleges and universities involve many constituent groups with divergent interests and values (Dressel, 1981; Glenny, 1979). As an integral part of an institution's planning process, the institutional research office can have considerable influence on its own destiny (Bryson and Howard, 1979).

In this chapter, an institutional fact book will be discussed both as a basic information system and as a practical communication vehicle. First, specific problems encountered in the use of large-scale, computer-based data files in the collegial planning of higher education will be explored. Next, an alternative method will be offered—the development and issuance of an annual institutional fact book. The fact book described was designed—and is acknowledged by users—to be the catalyst for effective application of institutional research at a state-supported university. An institutional research model, designed by this author and still evolving since its implementation in 1974, was adapted to the institution's own leadership, governing, and planning styles. Its strategy considers anticipation of needs, effectiveness of communication techniques, timeliness of information, and internal and external evaluations (Smith, 1980b). As background, the characteristics of this program are presented in Table 1. The program has two primary functions, to provide research and to serve as an information clearinghouse. Both functions will be shown to have influenced the design of the fact book as it relates to strategic planning.

Problems in Using a Management Information System (MIS)

Computer applications in postsecondary institutions have generated mountains of printouts, but the art of translating massive data into information that administrators and constituencies consider relevant remains difficult.

Table 1. Characteristics of the Institutional Research Program at Georgia State University

Primary Functions:	Research (communicative, conceptual, computer, and methodological skills), a practitioner's approach to studying the university and higher education. Universitywide information clearinghouse.
Primary Focus:	Largely a nonrepetitive process focusing on major questions of institutional direction, long-range strategies, and intra- and interinstitutional comparisons, both anticipated and requested.
Examples:	Source of analytical studies to provide a total institutional perspective (past, present, and future) dealing with students, faculty, staff, finances, programs, and purposes. Personnel serve as resource persons and consultants to central administration and university senate (verbal, graphic, and written presentations) to define problems and identify alternative courses, interpret data analyses for input into the planning process, review and digest higher education literature on major issues, and develop and implement minimodels for planning, including the institutional fact book.
Staff Members:	Eight, including professional (three), semiprofessional (four), and secretarial (one). Academic credentials concentrated in social sciences. Technical oriented semiprofessional staff with computer skills (two are half-time graduate students).

A review of MIS data from fifty institutions identified numerous problems. Entirely too much unfocused data were furnished, with no point of concentration. These frequent complaints indicated that the decision-making process was hindered by voluminous data reports (Baldridge, 1979, p. 271).

The notion that all items of hard data are factual information ignores the reality of any information's importance as a value judgment. Sound value judgments flow from combined wisdom and acute observations of a group process in which students, faculty members, trustees, and others often have a voice and a need for information. Problems with an academic MIS usually are caused by complex needs, diverse information users, and a tacit assumption and expectancy of hierarchical decision making. The success of a MIS depends on its capactiy to be integrated into the consensual decision-making process found in most colleges and universities (Schroeder and Adams, 1976). Marked differences between the processes of planning and decision making in business management and public administration (Drucker, 1974) account for satisfactory performance of an MIS in industry, but also for limitations in public higher education (Fincher, 1975; Gardner and Parker, 1978).

Higher education is administered in a political environment (Glenny, 1979; Moore, 1976; Walker, 1979a). This leadership style is frequently called participative, or collegial, management. It is often associated with a democratic governance process, a highly educated specialized work force, and a correspondingly weak hierarchical structure (Storrar, 1981). The nature of the organization and its environment determine whether administration or management is the most appropriate form of leadership. Moreover, the nature of the organization determines the appropriateness of information supplied by institutional research offices.

A political model is intrinsic to American public higher education. A university president has stated, "An approach to university administration based on the political patterns will more accurately predict organizational behaviors, will focus administrative effort on problem solving, and will yield better solutions to those problems. Whether we choose the political or some other model, the critical first step toward reality is to discard the pyramidal model. It is still there, overtly and covertly, coloring our views and confounding our attempts to understand campus events" (Walker, 1979b, p. 240). It may also be said that the political approach will tend to focus administrative effort on institutional research, as well.

To accumulate great masses of data is a rather useless endeavor, unless the effort is joined to a plan for transformation of "datamation" into information, with specific users in mind. A fact book is a framework for providing basic information, which supports strategic planning and, thus, problem solving. A regional survey of two- and four-year colleges found that academic administrators were acquainted with the concept of the MIS, but that the information system they actually used frequently and regularly was a fact book (Fincher and McCord, 1973). Of course, readily available and synthesized information is going to be used more than data files and printouts. A fact book has as many uses as staff members, resources, creativity, and ingenuity will permit (Leischuck, 1970).

The Fact Book as an Information System

Fact Book Example. The *Georgia State University Fact Book* is a bound document presenting a wide spectrum of descriptive information. The publication's editor designs a combination of useful, objective, and basic information to provide a concise overview of most facets of institutional operations. The editor recognizes the constituencies, depicts the dynamic environment of the organization, and meets the continuing need for information about this unique institution. Institutional facets inspiring high interest form the principal topic areas—institutional mission and strengths, organizational structure, students, faculty members, academic programs, financial resources, and physical facilities. Through systematic and timely distribution of the fact book, the publishers build confidence in the consistency of information about the whole institution. The book is in a ready and convenient form for users. It makes a significant contribution toward broad understanding of a complex organization (Smith, 1980a).

Production and Distribution Schedule. An awareness of and an active concern for the timeliness of a fact book prompts the schedule shown in Table 2. Out-of-date administrative data have limited applications except as historical

Table 2. Production and Distribution Schedule of an
Annual Institutional Fact Book

September 1	Editor establishes content of current issue and also gathers, organizes, and formats information. Art illustrator begins graphics. (Graphs are now prepared by the office of educational media and are based on projected fall-quarter data; the graphs prepared by the institutional research staff took approximately sixty hours to complete.)
October 1	Typist begins.
October 15	Fall-quarter enrollment report, reflecting official student counts prepared by registrar for state governing board, is received (example of the information clearinghouse activity). Data are extracted and graphed, mapped, and styled for fact book. Fall-quarter faculty data are retrieved by institutional research staff from computerized personnel-services and budget-data files and are then merged into an institutional-research computerized file and shaped for the fact book. This task is not performed specifically for the fact book, but serves many purposes—for example, annual faculty survey and most analytical studies of the faculty for a given year.
October 20	Typing and graphics completed and proofed, camera-ready copy delivered to the printer.
November 20	Fact book received from printer. Internal distribution is personalized with name labels. Distribution includes central administration, many levels of academic and student life, financial administrators, membership of the university senate, officers of the student government association, and student newspaper staff. The fact book is also placed in the library and filed with ERIC.
November 25	General distribution completed (bulk distribution made to some offices for specific groups—for example, state governing board, for officers and staff; alumni director, for alumni board; vice-president for urban affairs, for community and legislative use; research officer, for grant writers; development officer, for fundraising; public information officer, for public and external news media). Copies are mailed to the board of regents of the University System of Georgia, to presidents of the other thirty-three institutions comprising the University System of Georgia, and to two different peer groups with whom this institution exchanges information. By request, several external agencies have been added in recent years to the distribution list—Governor's Committee on Postsecondary Education, State Office of Planning and Budget, State Department of Labor, State Department of Industry and Trade, the Atlanta Chamber of Commerce, the Atlanta Budget and Planning Department, the Metropolitan Atlanta Rapid Transit Authority, and the Library of Congress.

archives. Often, ad hoc data from advanced computer technology cannot fulfill policy needs (Lasher, 1978); it is necessary to anticipate needs and demands to support planning. In each issue of the fact book, information on students and faculty members for the current fall quarter is included. Some information, particularly about finances, conforms to a fiscal-year basis for current and past years. Current information is thus provided that is useful for a full year. The fall-quarter distribution schedule eliminates many individual requests for information and largely accounts for the fact book's acceptance and popularity and for its multidimensional applications. The critical time schedule for information preparation and book distribution must be met to serve many of these needs.

Conceptual Design. The original fact book was designed to promote the wide usage and distribution shown in Table 2. The types of readers indicated would consider a fact book limited to tabular presentations of demographic statistics and output data as boring, unnecessary, and confusing.

Selecting components for the fact book focuses on information likely to be assimilated by institutional constituencies. This is necessary because generally accepted definitive guidelines are not available for higher education. The editor of the fact book encourages cooperative efforts toward information development. The most frequent questions asked about the institution by administrators, the faculty, students, and others are also used as indicators for information to be included in a given year. The editorship is not a perfunctory or isolated task; it involves cooperative and creative efforts, intuitive judgment, and knowledge of organizational behavior. The fact book also stimulates interactions with many offices and individuals. These continuing exchanges and user responses produce a climate in which it is possible to determine qualitatively how the publication is used within the university community and how it might better serve constituencies. A formal evaluation is sought every few years to ensure that the book's contents and methods respond to interests, needs, and demands.

Colleges and universities are complex organizations, and the information gathered must reflect this reality. The dynamic university environment is depicted by selecting and graphing relevant trend data on students, the faculty, programs, and finances. The environment is also depicted by selecting realistic pictorial illustrations to preface each of the major topical areas. The intent is to present a fact-based picture of the university. Logical organization, design, and layout are employed to assist diverse users. This style facilitates and accelerates comprehension by drawing on the reader's visual experience (Bowman, 1968; Dickerson, 1973). Mapping residential patterns of students and faculty members in the urban setting transforms massive zipcode data into interesting and useful demographic information. Such maps, developed jointly with the geography department, are examples of cooperative and creative efforts. Graphs and maps are visual and concise, making the publication economical to print and convenient to use.

Applications from Institutional Research Functions

Information Clearinghouse Applications. Individuals involved in operational activities at this university have cooperated in interoffice information exchanges through the years. In the absence of any formal universitywide system for information exchange, the institutional research function serves as an information clearinghouse (Bryson, 1977; Bryson and Posey, 1980). This effort ensures timeliness, consistency, and accuracy in external reporting. An added benefit to the institutional research office is the availability of diverse types of university data for various applications; the fact book is one example. The information clearinghouse function guarantees the availability of official data compilations that can be focused and condensed into widely shareable information. Figure 1, based on a data report of quarterly enrollment compiled for the state and federal governments, graphs the percentage distribution of students by class. It reflects congruence with the institutional role and mission; that is, the number of seniors and graduate students is disproportionately high when compared to the number of these students at a traditional university. This characteristic is readily apparent when graphed and would be obscured for many users if shown in tabular format.

Institutional Research Applications. Experience at our university has shown that analytical studies will be accepted and supported by the institution if needs for and uses of these studies are demonstrated. These studies are documented in written reports and are communicated through verbal, graphic, and written presentations to specific officers, faculty–administration groups,

Figure 1. Proportionate Distribution of Students by Class

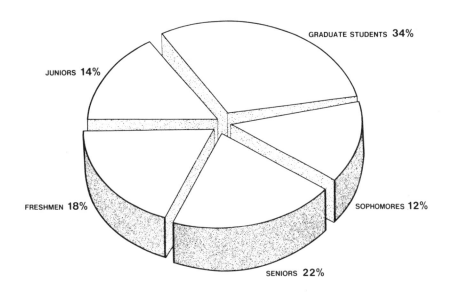

BY CLASS - Total Students N=20,333

or those charged to address major issues or accomplish strategic planning. The editor extracts highlights from certain studies that have widespread interest and policy implications; such studies have already been placed in the university library and may become the basis for professional papers or articles, through which external evaluations may be sought and received. Those studies chosen to be represented by one-page coverage in the fact book provide previously prepared materials and graphics for unifying through a widely shared publication. The fact book thus markets the institutional research function to a multilevel audience. Figure 2 illustrates a study condensation for this publication.

Strategic Planning Support

Institutional research reports can support, encourage, and facilitate planning. Consistent and widely shareable information, judged relevant by users, fosters consensus building based on mutual trust. Some specific applications of the fact book example are described and illustrated below.

Institutional Strengths. The annual distribution provides an opportunity for thousands of individuals to be informed about their institution. Figure 3 is a facsimile page featured prominently in a recent edition. It shows the profile of the institution. Opposite this page was shown a survey summary of perceptions of high school counselors throughout the state about this institution. Suitable for many audiences, such information has been used widely in news releases, brochures, and grant proposals; in public speeches by faculty and administrators; in briefings to legislative, alumni, and citizens' groups; and in freshman orientation by student inceptors. The public image promoted is that of a unique university forming an integral unit within a statewide system of higher education.

Self-Study for Reaffirmation of Accreditation. The fact book was identified as the primary support document for this lengthy and involved process. Four hundred committee members working throughout the university began the self-study process using identical universitywide information. The task of the institutional research office was to provide the information needed by these committees, which included faculty members, administrators, and students (Smith, 1980b). Anticipation of needs avoided fragmentation and duplication of efforts in preparing for an important coordinated visit by the regional accrediting association and ten programmatic agencies. The original design gives a source on each page, data definitions where needed, and a bibliography. This design, especially useful for the self-study, helps users locate more detailed information. In anticipation of the self-study, the editor incorporated some specific information suggested in the accreditation association's manual. Wide use of the fact book supported a unified self-study effort.

Physical Facilities. A critical need of this university is additional buildings. Its urban mission is to serve a working and commuting student popula-

Figure 2. Facsimile Page of the Condensation of a Study

GEORGIA STATE UNIVERSITY

IMPACT ON ATLANTA ECONOMY

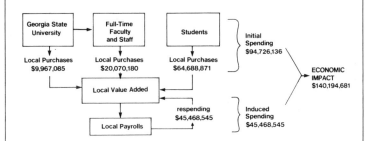

- In the course of pursuing its primary educational and cultural aims, Georgia State University provides the Atlanta community with a substantial extra dividend of jobs and income

- Forty-six percent of the students live in the Atlanta area largely because they are presently enrolled at Georgia State University

- The average student annually spends $7,307 in the local economy

- Faculty and staff members spend locally an average of $9,530 each

- The direct local purchases of the University amounted to $9,967,085 in fiscal 1978

- Direct spending from these three sources totaled $94,726,136. This figure is conservative since it omits spending by part-time employees and most part-time students

- But since each dollar of direct spending turns over several times in the 15-county Atlanta metropolitan area — an effect known as a "multiplier" — the total impact of Georgia State University was calculated at $140.2 million

- The University directly provided 2,106 full-time jobs and 1,522 part-time jobs in 1978. University-related spending generated an additional 3,326 full-time positions in the Atlanta community

- A noteworthy feature of this spending by Georgia State University is that it remains stable even through economic recession

SOURCE : Salley, C. D. Georgia State University Spending Patterns and the Atlanta Economy, 1978.
Institutional Research Report No. 79-8, Office of Institutional Planning, February, 1979.
ERIC Document No. ED 167 059

Figure 3. Facsimile Page Promoting the Public Image

GEORGIA STATE UNIVERSITY

PROFILE

- Georgia State University, a major public urban university in the nation, is a non-residential state-supported institution—a truly "urban university"
- The university is within an hour's commuting distance of two million citizens in the greater Atlanta area—one-third of the state's population
- The total full-time faculty numbers 856 for fall quarter. Three-fourths of the full-time teachers hold the doctorate; 69 percent are tenured; the average age is 43; and the average length of service is 8 years
- In an average quarter over 2,000 course sections are scheduled from 8 a.m. to 10 p.m., providing one of the most flexible academic time schedules in the country taught by a full-time faculty
- Degrees conferred during FY-80 totaled 3716
  - 112 doctorates
  - 133 specialists
  - 1565 masters
  - 1805 bachelors
  - 101 associates
- The six colleges and the Institute of Governmental Administration offer 46 degree programs with 197 areas of concentration
- During FY-80, 57,045 persons participated in 1,251 public service programs; in addition, speeches and presentations were delivered by faculty and staff members to approximately 150,000 persons

STUDENTS

- Enrollment for fall quarter, 1980, is 20,333—accounting for about one-tenth of all enrollees at accredited colleges in Georgia—both public and private
- Most Georgia State University students work while pursuing their studies (78 percent); 53 percent work full time and 25 percent part time
- The average age of undergraduate and graduate students is 25 and 31, respectively; the average age of all students is 27
- Women constitute the majority—accounting for 56 percent of the enrollees
- There are 1,226 veterans in attendance
- Nineteen percent of the students are minorities
- Graduate students make up one-third of the student body
- Residents of 72 foreign countries, all 50 states and the District of Columbia are attending the university as regular students
- Georgians comprise 93 percent of the total enrollment

Source: Coordinator of Institutional Research, October 1980

tion, and the complexities of classroom use seemed unintelligible to many influential constituent groups. Tabular data from a statewide room-utilization report would not have been able to clarify this need. The graphics shown in Figure 4 show the dynamics of classroom use as geared to a nontraditional scheduling pattern. Figure 4 was designed jointly by the offices of institutional research, educational media, and space management. Effectively communicating these space-use patterns was essential to the university's strategic planning, which culminated in the funding of several building projects in recent years. The annual visit by state funding officials coincides with the production schedule of the fact book. This scheduling permits up-to-date information, especially visuals, to be incorporated into the fact book.

Supporting strategic planning is rarely simple; there are no rules that ensure success. The main lessons we have learned from industry are that the planning process itself ought to change with the needs of the organization, that analytical tools can supplement but not supplant good thinking, and that a successful strategy cannot be developed without creative ideas at the beginning and management commitment at the end. In refining their sophisticated planning systems, many companies have become the victims of a "paralysis of analysis" (Hunsicker, 1980). Experience suggests that the content of a fact book ought to adapt to the changing planning needs of an institution. The planning emphasis may be stimulated, however, by innovative illustrations in the fact book.

The Fact Book as Catalyst

Consistent and widely shareable information judged relevant by users helps an institution to be understood, and this understanding is fundamental to planning. The fact book is a practical communication vehicle that serves as a basic information system. Developed by institutional research through cooperative efforts and from numerous available data sources, it unifies a wealth of information into a timely and convenient form for its diverse users. The intent to communicate the institution's reality to constituencies is demonstrated by content analysis, organization, editing, and thought. Selection of information for inclusion and communication not only is based on needs anticipation and responsiveness, but also is tempered by experience, insight, and understanding. Users value and assimilate information if its presentation is clear, concise, logical, and interesting.

Given the collegial nature of colleges and universities, such information sharing fosters mutual trust and is vital to group consensus. The type of publication described in this chapter can help an administration accomplish strategic planning. Examples have been presented here concerning institutional strengths and mission, the self-study process, and critical space needs to demonstrate the intricate ways in which the fact book supports planning. In this instance, it is the catalyst for an integrated institutional research program.

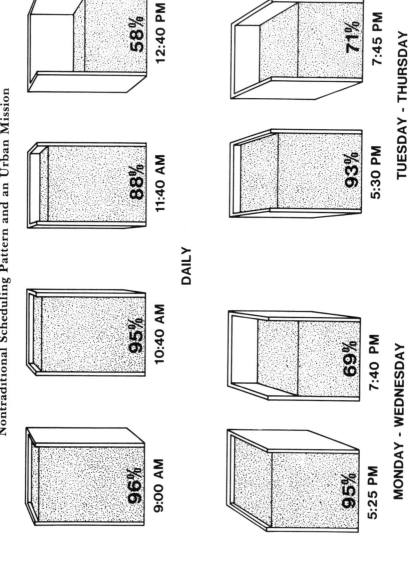

Figure 4. Dynamics of Classroom Space Utilization Geared to a Nontraditional Scheduling Pattern and an Urban Mission

DAILY

9:00 AM   96%   10:40 AM   95%   11:40 AM   88%   12:40 PM   58%

MONDAY - WEDNESDAY

5:25 PM   95%   7:40 PM   69%

TUESDAY - THURSDAY

5:30 PM   93%   7:45 PM   71%

Every institutional research report creates an image of this function. A high-quality fact book designates information that is clear because it is understandable to those who use it, timely because it gets to them when they need it, reliable because a diverse audience using the same publication sees it in the same way, valid because it captures reality by responding to its readers, adequate because the account is concise but judged relevant, and wide-ranging because the major facets of the institution are presented. A high-quality fact book also demonstrates the presence of a staff that has assimilated, organized, and communicated the facts. These fundamental characteristics can play a pivotal role and gain broad-based acceptance and support for the institutional research office. The demands of timeliness, creativity, and effective communication are challenges that institutional research must meet in order to be channeled into the institutional mainstream of decision making, policy formulation, and planning.

References

Arns, R. G. "Organizational Characteristics of a University: Implications for Design and Use of Information Systems." *CAUSE/EFFECT,* 1979, *2* (5), 26–33.

Baldridge, J. V. "Impacts on College Administration: Management Information Systems and Management-by-Objective Systems." *Research in Higher Education,* 1979, *10,* 263–282.

Bowman, W. J. *Graphic Communication.* New York: Wiley, 1968.

Bryson, C. H. "The Institutional Research Office: Report Factory or Information Clearinghouse?" In R. H. Fenske (Ed.), *Research and Planning for Higher Education.* Tallahassee, Fla.: Association for Institutional Research, 1977.

Bryson, C. H., and Howard, R. D. "A Call for Different Styles of Data Management and Institutional Research: Centralized Versus Decentralized Planning." *CAUSE/ EFFECT,* 1979, *2* (2), 10–15.

Bryson, C. H., and Posey, E. I. "Statewide Data Systems: Some Policy Questions in an Era of Financial Retrenchment." *CAUSE/EFFECT,* 1980, *3* (4), 18–23.

Dickerson, G. C. *Statistical Mapping and the Presentation of Statistics.* New York: Crane, Russak and Company, 1973.

Dressel, P. L. "The Shaping of Institutional Research and Planning." *Research in Higher Education,* 1981, *14,* 229–258.

Drucker, P. F. *Management: Tasks, Responsibilities, Practices.* New York: Harper & Row, 1974.

Fincher, C. "Grand Strategy and the Failure of Consensus." *Educational Record,* 1975, *56,* 10–20.

Fincher, C. "On Professional Meetings and Publication." *Research in Higher Education,* 1979, *10* (1), 3–9.

Fincher, C., and McCord, M. *Management Concepts in Academic Administration.* Athens: University of Georgia Institute of Higher Education, 1973.

Gardner, D. E., and Parker, J. D. "MIS in Higher Education: A Reassessment." *CAUSE/EFFECT,* 1978, *1* (3), 10–13, 16–17.

Glenny, L. "The Anonymous Leaders of Higher Education." *Journal of Higher Education,* 1979, *50* (4), 400–412.

Hunsicker, J. Q. "The Malaise of Strategic Planning." *Management Review,* 1980, *69* (3), 8–14.

Lasher, W. F. "The Comprehensive Institutional Planning Process and the Role of Information in It." *Planning for Higher Education,* 1978, *6* (4), 11–15.

Leischuck, G. S. "Communicating the Results of Institutional Research: The Production and Uses of the Fact Book." In P. S. Wright (Ed.), *Institutional Research and Communication in Higher Education.* Tallahassee, Fla.: Association for Institutional Research, 1970.

Moore, J. "Pragmatic Considerations in Academic Planning." *Planning for Higher Education,* 1976, *6,* 3–5.

Past Presidents' Panel. "AIR in the Eighties." In P. J. Staskey (Ed.), *Annual Forum Proceedings No. 2: Issues for the Eighties.* Tallahassee, Fla.: Association for Institutional Research, 1979.

Patrick, C., and Caruthers, J. K. "Management Priorities of College Presidents." *Research in Higher Education,* 1980, *12* (3), 195–214.

Schroeder, R. G., and Adams, C. R. "The Effective Use of Management Science in University Administration." *Review of Educational Research,* 1976, *46* (1), 117–131.

Smith, G. "Systematic Information Sharing in Participative University Management." *Journal of Higher Education,* 1980a, *51* (5), 519–526.

Smith, G. "Visibility and Viability of Institutional Research." Paper presented at the meeting of the Southern Association for Institutional Research, Louisville, Ky., October 1980b.

Storrar, S. J. "Perceptions of Organizational and Political Environments: Results of a National Survey of Institutional Research/Planning Officers at Large Public Universities." Paper presented at the Association for Institutional Research forum, Minneapolis/St. Paul, May 1981.

Walker, D. E. *The Effective Administrator.* San Francisco: Jossey-Bass, 1979a.

Walker, D. E. "University Administration on a Political Model." *Educational Record,* 1979b, *60* (3), 234–240.

Glynton Smith directs the institutional research program at
Georgia State University. She has served as a state, regional,
and national workshop leader and consultant and has published articles
about fact book development and about the institutional research program
that has been described in this chapter. She has received two
Sidney Suslow awards honoring her institutional research efforts.

A technique for use in any phase of planning
where convergence of opinion seems desirable is described,
along with its limitations and the methodological problems
that may arise with its use.

Using the Delphi Technique in Institutional Planning

Norman P. Uhl

Decision making is often difficult and frustrating in the academic world. This is particularly true if a decison requires the approval and cooperation of a collective group such as the faculty, department heads, deans, and so forth. Such decisions, if they are to be successfully implemented, require prior agreement among the members of these groups. Unfortunately, agreement usually is hindered by great divergences of opinion, strong allegiances, and the varying vested interests that frequently characterize these groups. A technique that can be used not only to help overcome such difficulties but also to assist in arriving at collective decisions is the subject of this chapter. It is known as the Delphi technique. In its earlier use, the Delphi technique was considered to be primarily a method for forecasting the future, and it is still frequently used in this manner. Nevertheless, its great potential for improving communication and generating consensus in solving complex problems is beginning to be realized.

General Background

It is interesting that the Delphi method receives its name from early Greek mythology. Delphi, famous as a center of wealth and wisdom and as the seat of culture and learning in ancient Greece, was the hallowed sanctuary of

N. P. Uhl (Ed.). *Using Research for Strategic Planning.* New Directions for Institutional Research, no. 37. San Francisco: Jossey-Bass, March 1983.

Apollo and the most revered of the ancient Greek oracles. It was from Delphi that Apollo's predictions or forecasts were transmitted to those who sought to hear them. Thus, down through the centuries, the name Delphi has been associated with forecasts of the future.

The Delphi process is a procedure originally developed by the RAND Corporation for obtaining greater consensus among experts regarding urgent defense problems, without face-to-face discussion. While face-to-face discussion is the usual procedure for combining individual opinions, it has been recognized for about twenty-five years that there are serious problems associated with this mode of communication (Asch, 1958; Kelly and Thibaut, 1954). Some of these problems can be stated in the following ways.

1. While group opinion is highly influenced by dominant individuals, who usually monopolize a discussion, there is little correlation between verbosity and knowledge of the subject matter under consideration.

2. Much discussion in group situations, while appearing to be problem-oriented, is either irrelevant or biased, because it is usually more concerned with individual and group interests than with problem solving.

3. Individual judgment can be distorted by group pressure to conform.

The objective of the Delphi technique is to obtain convergence of opinion without bringing individuals together in face-to-face meetings. This objective is usually achieved by having the participants complete a series of questionnaires interspersed with controlled opinion feedback. This mode of controlled interaction among the respondents not only means savings in time and money, but also permits independent thought among participants and assists them in the gradual formation of a considered opinion. It has the added advantage of ensuring participants' anonymity. Direct confrontation, in contrast, as experienced in faculty or committee meetings, often results in hasty offering of preconceived notions, the inclination to close one's mind to novel ideas, a tendency to defend previously taken stands, and a tendency to be influenced by the persuasively stated opinions of others.

The general procedure for the Delphi technique is as follows:

1. The participants are asked to list their opinions on a specific topic such as curriculum revision or planning priorities.

2. The participants are then asked to evaluate the total list by a criterion such as importance, chance of success, and so on.

3. The participants receive the list and a summary of responses to the items. If the participants are in the minority, they are asked to revise their opinions or indiciate their reasons for remaining in the minority.

4. The participants again receive the list, an updated summary, minority opinions, and another chance to revise their opinions.

Since the mid-1960s, the Delphi technique has been used in business, government, industry, medicine, regional planning, and education over a wide variety of situations, including futures forecasting, goal assessment, curriculum planning, establishment of budget priorities, estimates concerning the quality of life, policy formulation, and problem identification and formulation of solutions. Linstone and Turoff (1975), in their compendium on the Delphi method, describe many of the studies performed in areas other than education. Unfortunately, the better-known bibliographies on the Delphi method include very few applications to education, much less to higher education. For example, the RAND Corporation's listing (RAND Corporation, 1971) includes one reference related to education out of forty-one listed references. In spite of this shortage, it would be erroneous to conclude that few studies have been conducted in higher education using the Delphi technique. It is interesting to note, however, that the publication of Delphi studies in the field of higher education seems to have peaked in the early mid-1970s, and since 1976 a reduction in published studies has occurred. This does not necessarily mean that studies have not been performed recently; it means only that fewer are being reported in professional journals, which is not surprising when we consider that, in more recent years, the Delphi technique has been used less as a forecasting tool than as a method of improving communication. This latter use frequently involves the investigation of sensitive issues. Consequently, institutions may not wish to publicize their results. Uhl (1971), Judd (1972), Huckfeldt and Judd (1975), and Peterson and Uhl (1977) all refer to numerous studies in higher education that have employed the Delphi technique.

Huckfeldt and Judd (1975) divide the Delphi studies in higher education into five major areas, each of which is briefly discussed below. In general, the studies referred to contain sufficient detail to assist readers who may be contemplating similar investigations.

Cost-Effectiveness. Very little has been done in this area. Reisman (1969) used the Delphi technique in determining a budget, and Mantel and Service (1975) employed it as a social service measurement model.

Curriculum Planning. While the Delphi technique has been employed by many institutions to assist in curriculum planning and revision, institutions are unlikely to publish these types of studies. Nevertheless, an excellent account of how a curriculum was developed for a new branch campus through the use of the Delphi technique is described by Judd (1971). Rossman and Bunning (1978) investigated the skills that adult education would require in the future. Reeves and Jauch (1978) also describe a curriculum development project that used the Delphi technique.

Goals. Many studies have been performed in this area. Uhl's (1970, 1971) study in 1969 of the goals of five quite different postsecondary education institutions was one of the first performed on identifying goals and obtained excellent return rates from diverse constituent groups, as well as convergence of opinion about most goals on each campus. It differed from many other studies, in that it used an early form of the *Institutional Goals Inventory* on the first round, rather than free-response questions. Uhl (1971) provides a detailed chronological account of the procedure used in the 1969 study. Huckfeldt and Judd (1975) emphasize the Delphi process itself and offer a number of suggestions for conducting such studies. The School of Education at the University of Virginia (Cyphert and Gant, 1971) conducted a Delphi study to assess the needs, desires, and opinions of different clientele, from which findings the institution could re-examine its goals. Hudspeth (1970) describes a statewide Delphi study to acquire insight into the goals of higher education.

Rating Scales. Fox and Brookshire (1971) used the Delphi technique to obtain agreement among faculty on what should be considered effective college teaching.

Forecasts of the Future. The National Center for Higher Education Management Systems (NCHEMS) study of changes in postsecondary education (Huckfeldt, 1972) is an example of a large Delphi study. Adams's (1980) study of future issues in grievance arbitration applies the Delphi technique to a current topic.

Uses of the Delphi Technique in Planning

While the Delphi technique is a popular tool, care must be taken not to let the technique determine the problem. The use of the Delphi technique may be warranted if any or all of the following conditions exist: (1) the resolution of a problem can be facilitated by the collective judgments of one or more groups; (2) those groups providing judgments are unlikely to communicate adequately without an intervening process; (3) the solution is more likely to be accepted if more people are involved in its development than would be possible in a face-to-face meeting; (4) frequent group meetings are not practical because of time, distance, and so forth; and (5) one or more groups of participants are more dominant than another. For the most extensive critique of the Delphi process itself, see Sackman (1974); for a rebuttal, see Coates (1975).

The above five conditions can occur in any of the four planning phases: the analysis phase, the mission-and-goals phase, the objectives and action-plans phase, and the resource-use, needs-analysis, and expenditure-strategies phase. For example, in the analysis phase, the Delphi technique commonly has been employed to forecast the future. It can also be used to assess the internal environment and to determine solutions to existing problems. This latter use of the Delphi technqiue has great potential, but studies using it in this way in higher education have rarely been published. Uhl (1981) performed such a study, in which solutions were sought to racial problems at a high school. The first round of questions was open-ended and asked students, parents, teachers, and administrators to identify the problems. The second round listed the identified problems and asked the participants to indicate the degree of importance of each problem and, if possible, to suggest a solution. The third round listed several solutions to each of the problems and requested the participants to rate each solution on a scale of one (not a solution) to five (excellent solution). On the next round, the most frequently selected solution for each problem was circled, and the respondents were asked again to rate the solutions. If they did not agree that a circled solution was the best, they were asked to provide reasons for their disagreement. In the last round, these reasons for disagreement were distributed, with another request to rate the solutions. It was interesting to find strong agreement on one or two solutions to each problem. The very small amount of disagreement on solutions that did exist on the last round was found to be more within the same group than between different groups (racial groups, for example). This same technique can be employed on a campus to identify solutions to such possible problems as student attrition, campus morale, or office efficiency. Through this procedure, perceived weaknesses and possible solutions can be identified with regard to almost any aspect of an institution's internal environment.

In the second planning phase, which involves mission and goal identification and agreement, the Delphi technique has already made a significant contribution, as mentioned earlier. Another important part of this planning phase is goal evaluation, which can employ a technique similar to the one used for solving racial problems, described above, or the technique used in the studies involving rating scales.

The development of objectives and action plans is the third planning phase, and again, the Delphi technique may be applicable; certainly, ways of achieving high-priority goals can be the subject of a Delphi study. It may be necessary to limit the scope of the study, since it would be neither expected nor necessarily good for all units to have the same action plans for achieving the same goal. We would expect academic departments and admissions offices to have quite different but equally valid approaches to the same goal. Thus, a Delphi study in this phase would usually involve one, two, or possibly a few units, but not necessarily the whole campus.

The last planning phase is the resource-use, needs-analysis, and expenditure-strategies phase. There is no question that the Delphi technique can be useful in helping establish priorities. Thus, the Delphi technique is applicable in any of the planning phases, but it should be used only when needed, since it will consume time and resources.

Forecasting Versus Other Uses

Forecasting the future involves quite different thinking than developing solutions to present problems, identifying current goals, or establishing priorities, yet the Delphi technique has been used in higher education in both ways, without much consideration for these differences. It is important to understand that these differences do affect the design of the Delphi study itself. For this reason, forecasting will be discussed separately from other uses of the Delphi.

Forecasting. Although the Delphi technique was used originally as a forecasting tool, it should be emphasized that, when used for this purpose, the

Delphi technique has definite weaknesses. As Weaver (1971) indicates, the Delphi technique assumes that experts, because they are objective, take new information into account and construct logically sound deductions about the future, based on thorough and disciplined understanding of particular phenomena and how they are related. When we consider that most forecasts are not concerned with projections, but, rather, with quantum leaps into the future, it is questionable that even experts can respond on the basis of sound deductive reasoning. Since the experts' reasoning is not requested in most Delphi studies, there is no way to check the plausibility of the experts' responses. As possible users or consumers of this method of forecasting, institutional researchers should understand this possible bias and the procedures that can be employed to reduce it. While bias can arise from the situation and the researcher, in forecasting studies bias from the respondent is more serious.

To examine the bias of the respondent, it is necessary to determine whether intentions or opinions are being requested. *Intentions* refer to a person's planned behavior, which is within the individual's control. In contrast, *opinions* refer to circumstances external to the individual and over which the individual exercises little or no control. For example, the chairperson of a department may have the intention to offer a new degree program in the department; the same individual may have the opinion that the rate of inflation will decrease. Whether or not the individual has some control over circumstances determines the classification of his or her activity or remarks as intention or opinion.

When intentions are requested in a forecasting study, the degree to which useful information will be obtained is directly related to six questions:

1. How important is the event to the respondent? (The greater the importance of the topic to the respondent, the more confident the user can be of the prediction. For example, intentions will provide good predictions for the respondent's choice of occupation, not so good predictions for choice of geographical area to work in, and poor predictions for the type of watch the individual will be wearing.)

2. Who are the appropriate decision makers, and how willing are they to participate in the study? (The greater the participation of appropriate decision makers, the better their predictions.)

3. Do the above participants already have a plan? (The more formalized the plan, the better the predictions.)

4. Are the participants willing to publicize their plan? (If the plan depends on secrecy for its effectiveness, the participant is less likely to offer predictions based on the plan.)

5. Do the participants have the authority to carry out the plan? (The more responsibility the participants have for the plan, the better the predictions.)

6. Is there unlikelihood of a change in plans as a result of new information? (The less likely a change in plans, the more accurate the predictions.)

If most of the conditions reflected in these six questions can be achieved in a study, then good predictions should result from using intentions. In most situations, however, very few if any of the conditions can be met, and therefore opinions, not intentions, should be requested.

When opinions are requested, there are several points to consider in designing the study:

1. Participants' responses reflect not only what they think will occur, but also what they hope will occur. Therefore, the greater the participant's involvement in the forecast situation, the greater the expected bias.

2. Many participants assume that the future will resemble the past — that is, they find it difficult to envision abrupt changes.

3. While the participants' expertise in the subject being forecast can be of value in assessing current status, expertise beyond a minimal level is of no value in making predictions. Therefore, one should use the least expensive experts who are willing to participate. Several studies support this point (Granger and Morgenstern, 1970; Richards, 1976; Taft, 1955).

4. Experts should be used who have differing views on important variables related to the forecast.

5. More than ten experts are unnecessary for opinion data. This guideline is in contrast to those for intentions data, where random sampling should be employed.

6. One should provide only the minimum relevant information to the expert. Tversky and Kahneman (1974) have shown that people have a tendency to ignore prior probabilities when worthless or irrelevant information is added (that is, when the situation is made complex).

7. If a response scale is used, one with seven, nine, or eleven points is preferable; five is acceptable.

8. Open-ended questions should be considered for sensitive issues.

Studies that have additional methodological implications for forecasting include Chaffin and Talley (1980), Dodge and Clark (1977), Martino (1970), Salancik (1973), and Salancik, Wenger, and Helfer (1971).

In summary, the Delphi technique is one method for assessing the future; it is not necessarily the best. For a discussion of different forecasting procedures, see the *Handbook of Futures Research* (Fowles, 1978). It should be remembered that the method best suited to the problem should be selected, not the problem best suited to the method. If the Delphi technique is chosen, the considerations discussed above can be used for designing the study.

Delphi Uses Other Than Forecasting. In contrast to studies in which forecasting the future is the objective of using the Delphi technique, the primary purpose of other Delphi studies is to communicate and obtain convergence of opinion. Whether the study is being used to establish priorities, plan a curriculum, identify important goals, or develop solutions to particular problems, one of the usual goals is to reach some agreement among the participants. While studies have shown that agreement usually occurs, it cannot be guaranteed. Uhl (1971) obtained agreement among faculty, administrators, students, parents, the governing board, alumni, and a group of community leaders on the importance of most of the goals at five different institutions. At each institution, agreement was not obtained on two or three of the twenty goal areas. The few goal areas where agreement was not achieved generally differed for the five institutions. In addition, Uhl found that agreement was easier to obtain on items that requested the respondent's perception of an existing situation (How important is this goal?) than on items requesting a value judgment (How important should the goal be?). Present perceptions usually converged to agreement one round before the value judgments converged. In examining this finding, it was found that respondents who were less familiar with the campus (alumni, governing board, community leaders, parents) tended to change their perceptions of the present campus to agree more with the group median. This is not surprising, since the off-campus groups would expect the faculty, administrators, and students to know more about the present campus. When value judgments were requested, however, it was not possible to predict which groups would change their original perceptions. It seems that off-campus groups considered their opinions about what "should be" to be as valuable as any other group's opinions. Nevertheless, even with value judgments, convergence occurred in almost all cases, but an additional round of communication was usually needed.

In nonforecasting studies, the selection of experts is not a real concern. The participants are selected from those groups that need to communicate and be part of the decision-making process. Thus, the determination of who participates is a political, governance-type decision.

For those who may be considering this type of study, a set of short planning guidelines is presented here:

1. Be certain there is not a simpler and less costly procedure that will achieve the same results.
2. Do not underestimate the time and resources needed to provide the necessary feedback.
3. Select the participants with care and in a manner consistent with the objective of the study.
4. Use unambiguous statements, neither too vague nor too specific, to obtain valid and efficient input from participants.
5. Do not mislead the participants.
6. Do not ignore the responses of participants who disagree with the majority.
7. Do not impose the views and biases of the study designers on the participants.
8. Allow enough time between rounds to prepare and distribute feedback, but do not allow so much time that participants lose interest in the study.
9. Provide participants with enough incentive to remain interested throughout the study.

Conducting the Delphi Study

The major steps in conducting the Delphi study include delineating the project's purposes, establishing a Delphi project committee, delineating the project's scope, beginning the study (Round Zero), developing the Round One questionnaire, analyzing the Round One content, processing Round Two, processing Round Three and succeeding rounds, and using the results.

Delineating the Project's Purposes. While there is usually one major purpose for the study, there may also be some others that are vaguely defined. If so, they should be clarified so that everyone involved in the planning of the study will be aware of all the purposes. If this step is done well, the next two steps will be made easier.

Establishing a Delphi Project Committee. After the purposes of the study have been identified, it will be helpful to establish a committee to help the institutional researcher conduct the study. This committee should be composed of people who will lend credibility to the study. They will help determine the scope of the study and react to drafts of questionnaires and reports. Throughout the Delphi process, it is very important that the person conducting the study be perceived by the participants as fair and neutral on the issues if the group is to have confidence in the results (Hartman, 1981).

Delineating the Project's Scope. The basic questions are which groups to include and what size samples to use. The answers will depend on the purpose(s) of the study. If the purpose is to revise an undergraduate curriculum, then undergraduate faculty members, students, and certain administrators may be involved. Depending on the study and the political situation, it may be useful to include a sample of alumni and members of the governing board. The sample size also depends on the purposes of the study. One should be aware that the larger the sample, the more time-consuming the data analysis will be for each round. Samples should be used whenever possible, but if the results must be voted on or implemented by the faculty of a particular school, then it may be worth the extra analysis time to include the entire faculty of that school. If the faculty has had a part in arriving at the decision, the decision is more likely to be acceptable.

If subgroups are to be compared, it is important to obtain enough responses; the exact number will be determined separately for each subgroup. For example, if twelve of the thirty members of a governing board received questionnaires and ten completed them, this would be considered an adequate response rate. If only ten out of a hundred faculty members returned completed questionnaires, it would be a very inadequate response rate.

In determining the sample size to use with each group, it is necessary to consider the expected response rate. As experienced institutional researchers know, 100 percent respondent cooperation can seldom be expected. With well-laid groundwork and a climate of acceptance for the project, response rates as high as 80 to 90 percent have been attained (Uhl, 1971), but campuses and situations differ. Institutional researchers can judge what to expect on the basis of past experience.

Beginning the Study (Round Zero). Round Zero refers to work done before distributing the first questionnaires and is the single most important step. A useful procedure that can greatly decrease the number of nonreturns and generally improve the study is to invite potential panel members to participate. Those who agree to participate are more likely to continue throughout the study. If some do not agree to participate, there is time at this stage to substitute someone else. It is also possible to send a short questionnaire to those who have refused and determine whether or not they differ in important ways from those who are participating. This information will assist later decisions about whether the participants are representative of the groups from which they were selected.

The invitation to participate should be made by someone whom the individuals respect, should indicate the importance of the study, and should be personally addressed. Members of different groups may be sent slightly different letters, as a way of appealing to their particular interests.

At this stage, it is important to develop a realistic schedule for the project and decide how the data analysis and synthesis of responses will be performed. The time needed to distribute the questionnaires, complete them, and have them returned must be carefully considered. It is reasonable to ask participants to complete questionnaires within five days. If more time is given, participants may tend to delay and may never complete the questionnaires. Sufficient time should be allowed for returning the questionnaires. Some studies have reported that three weeks between rounds is adequate (Huckfeldt, 1972; Uhl, 1971), but this estimate assumes that computer programs or other data-processing methods will be developed and checked prior to starting the first round.

While anonymity should be preserved, in certain studies of methodology it may be desirable to track an individual's responses on all rounds. One method of accomplishing this step is to attach a cover page to the questionnaire on which individual participants write their names. When the questionnaire is returned, a number is placed on it to identify the respondent, and the cover page is removed. Other procedures work equally well. With sensitive issues, however, it may not be possible to request names, even using techniques such as those described above, without affecting the data.

Developing the Round One Questionnaire. The traditional Delphi study is characterized by a first round in which the participants have an opportunity to provide free responses to rather unstructured questions. For example,

1. List the most important goals for our institution.

2. Describe some interractial problems you have observed or heard about at _____ High School, and suggest what could be done to solve these problems or to avoid similar ones in the future [Uhl, 1974].

In some instances, as in the first example, some desirable statements may be overlooked by the participants, and/or the responses of the participants will be so different that the compilation of statements for the next round will be very difficult and time-consuming.

An alternate approach is to skip the first round and provide a structured questionnaire. If this approach were used to identify the goals of an institution, a long list of goals would be provided for the participants, who would be asked to indicate their importance on a five-, seven-, nine-, or eleven-point scale. By leaving space for the participants to modify statements or add goals that they believe are important, researchers can elicit additional goals considered important by the participants. Uhl (1971) followed this approach, using the *Institutional Goals Inventory* as the list of goals. This procedure was less frustrating for participants and ensured that a wide range of goals would be considered. Delphi studies using these two different approaches indicate that researchers can expect a much higher participant dropout rate with the unstructured questions than with the structured questions. Therefore, there are some specific advantages of providing a more structured questionnaire, if it does not seriously limit participants' responses. When this procedure is followed, it is technically Round Two; therefore, the processing of the data is described under "Processing Round Two" (below).

Unfortunately, there are situations when not enough is known to provide the structured questionnaire and it will be necessary to request free responses; the second example (above) indicates such a situation. In either situation, the questionnaire should be pretested with the Delphi committee, as well as with individuals who are members of the groups participating in the study, but who are not themselves study participants.

Analyzing Round One Content. Analyzing responses to unstructured questions is an important but difficult task. Professionals familiar with the subject matter should perform this task, since it involves synthesizing all responses into one list. Difficult decisions have to be made constantly, and it is a very time-consuming process. Huckfeldt and Judd (1975) describe their procedure for such a content analysis.

Processing Round Two. When a structured questionnaire is used, analysis is rather straightforward. The main objectives are to provide feedback and add to the list anything written in by participants, so that these additions can be considered on the next round. It takes little time, and usually very few decisions have to be made. Feedback to each item should be provided regarding the measure of central tendency to be employed. The most frequently used statistics are the overall group mode or median. Some researchers also indicate the individual's previous response, but this requires additional work, which many researchers consider unnecessary. This same analysis procedure is applicable to the structured questions developed from the content analysis of the Round One free-response questionnaire. As before, the new instrument should be pretested.

Processing Round Three and Succeeding Rounds. Again, the overall group statistics for each item or question are calculated and then fed back to the participants. On Round Three, participants have also provided reasons for disagreement with the modal or median response for each item. These minority views must be reviewed, synthesized, and distributed on the next round, so that participants can read them before answering the questions. The processing is repeated with each successive round. Scheibe, Skutsch, and Shofer (1975) and Uhl (1971) report that three rounds are usually sufficient to obtain convergence of opinion.

Using the Results. If a Delphi study is performed, the results should be used for whatever purpose was intended. If the results are not used, the participants may return to their Round One opinions. In a follow-up of a Delphi study at an institution where the results had not been used, Uhl (1975) found that faculty responses were closer one year later to their Round One responses than to their Round Three responses. At an institution where the results were used and widely publicized, the opposite seemed to occur: faculty members seemed closer to their responses on the last round than to their Round One responses.

Summary

The Delphi technique, while not highly recommended for forecasting, is a useful communication tool, which institutional researchers can use to assist all phases of planning. Researchers interested in performing such a study should be aware of certain specific guidelines to be used in the design and implementation of the Delphi technique.

References

Adams, L. A. "Delphi Forecasting: Future Issues in Grievance Arbitration." *Technological Forecasting and Social Change,* 1980, *18,* 151–160.

Asch, S. E. "Effects of Group Pressure upon the Modification and Distortion of Judgments." In E. E. Maccoby, T. M. Newcomb, and E. L. Hartley (Eds.), *Readings in Social Psychology.* (3rd ed.) London: Holt, Rinehart and Winston, 1958.

Chaffin, W. W., and Talley, W. "Individual Stability in Delphi Studies." *Technological Forecasting and Social Change,* 1980, *16,* 67–73.

Coates, J. F. "Review of Sackman Report." *Technological Forecasting and Social Change,* 1975, *7* (2), 193–194.

Cyphert, F. R., and Gant, W. L. "The Delphi Technique: A Case Study." *Phi Delta Kappan,* 1971, *52,* 272–273.

Dodge, B. J., and Clark, R. E. "Research on the Delphi Technique." *Educational Technology,* 1977, *17,* 58–60.

Fowles, J. *Handbook of Futures Research.* Westport, Conn.: Greenwood Press, 1978.

Fox, A. M, and Brookshire, W. K. "Defining Effective College Teaching." *The Journal of Experimental Education,* 1971, *40* (2), 37–40.

Granger, C. W. J., and Morgenstern, O. *Predictability of Stock Market Prices.* Lexington, Mass.: Heath, 1970.

Hartman, A. "Reaching Consensus Using the Delphi Technique." *Educational Leadership*, 1981, *38*, 495–497.

Huckfeldt, V. E. *A Forecast of Changes in Postsecondary Education.* Boulder, Colo.: National Center for Higher Education Management Systems, 1972.

Huckfeldt, V. E., and Judd, R. C. *Methods for Large-Scale Delphi Studies.* Boulder, Colo.: National Center for Higher Education Management Systems, 1975.

Hudspeth, D. R. *A Long-Range Planning Tool for Education: The Focus Delphi.* Syracuse, N.Y.: Syracuse University Research Institute, 1970.

Judd, R. C. "Delphi Applications for Decision Making." *Planning and Changing*, 1971, *2*, 151–156.

Judd, R. C. "Forecasting to Consensus Gathering: Delphi Grows Up to College Needs." *College and University Business*, 1972, *53*, 35–43.

Kelly, H. H., and Thibaut, J. W. "Experimental Studies of Group Problem Solving and Process." In G. Lindzey (Ed.), *Handbook of Social Psychology.* Vol. 2. Reading, Mass.: Addison-Wesley, 1954.

Linstone, H. A., and Turoff, M. *The Delphi Method: Techniques and Applications.* Reading, Mass.: Addison-Wesley, 1975.

Mantel, S. J., and Service, A. L. "A Social Service Measurement Model." *Operations Research*, 1975, *23* (2), 218–239.

Martino, J. "The Precision of Delphi Estimates." *Technological Forecasting and Social Change*, 1970, *1*, 293–299.

Peterson, R. E., and Uhl, N. P. *Formulating College and University Goals.* Princeton, N.J.: Educational Testing Service, 1977.

RAND Corporation. *Selected RAND Publications—Delphi.* Santa Monica, Calif.: The RAND Corporation, 1971.

Reeves, G., and Jauch, L. R. "Curriculum Development Through Delphi." *Research in Higher Education*, 1978, *8* (2), 157–168.

Reisman, A. *Evaluation and Budgeting Model for a System of Social Agencies.* Technical Memorandum No. 167. Cleveland, Ohio: Case Western Reserve University, 1969.

Richards, R. M. "Analysts' Performance and the Accuracy of Corporate Earnings Forecasts." *Journal of Business*, 1976, *49*, 350–357.

Rossman, M. H., and Bunning, R. L. "Knowledge and Skills for the Adult Educator: A Delphi Study." *Adult Education*, 1978, *28* 139–155.

Sackman, H. *Delphi Assessment: Expert Opinion, Forecasting, and Group Process.* Santa Monica, Calif.: The RAND Corporation, 1974.

Salancik, J. R. "Assimilation of Aggregated Inputs into Delphi Forecasts: A Regression Analysis." *Technological Forecasting and Social Change*, 1973, *5* (3), 243–248.

Salancik, J. R., Wenger, W., and Helfer, E. "The Construction of Delphi Event Statements." *Technological Forecasting and Social Change*, 1971, *3* (1), 65–73.

Scheibe, M., Skutsch, M., and Shofer, J. "Experiments in Delphi Methodology." In H. A. Linstone and M. Turoff (Eds.), *The Delphi Method: Techniques and Applications.* Reading, Mass.: Addison-Wesley, 1975.

Taft, R. "The Ability to Judge People." *Psychological Bulletin*, 1955, *52*, 1–28.

Tversky, A., and Kahneman, D. "Judgment Under Uncertainty: Heuristics and Biases." *Science*, 1974, *27*, 1124–1131.

Uhl, N. P. "A Technique for Improving Communication Within an Institution." In P. Wright (Ed.), *Institutional Research and Communication in Higher Education.* Tallahassee, Fla.: Association for Institutional Research, 1970.

Uhl, N. P. *Identifying Institutional Goals.* Durham, N.C.: National Laboratory for Higher Education, 1971. (ERIC/ED 049713)

Uhl, N. P. "A Procedure for Identifying Problems and Solutions in Desegregated Schools." Paper presented at the annual meeting of the American Educational Research Association, Chicago, April 1974.

Uhl, N. P. "A Follow-Up of a Delphi Study." Paper presented at the annual forum of the Association for Institutional Research, May 1975.

Uhl, N. P. "An Action-Oriented Technique for Improving a Campus Environment." In J. Smith (Ed.), *The Impact of Desegregation on Higher Education.* Durham, N.C.: North Carolina Central University Institute on Desegregation, 1981.

Weaver, W. T. "The Delphi Forecasting Method." *Phi Delta Kappan,* 1971, *52,* 267–271.

Norman P. Uhl is professor of education at Mount Saint Vincent University in Halifax, Nova Scotia. Previously, he was associate vice-chancellor for research, evaluation, and planning at North Carolina Central University and research psychologist with Educational Testing Service. He is coauthor of the Institutional Goals Inventory.

This chapter contains a discussion of the implications
of developing a closer relationship between institutional research
and planning. Additional sources of Canadian research and futures research
are also provided.

Conclusions and Additional Sources

Norman P. Uhl
Anne Marie MacKinnon

Effective strategic planning depends on the availability of appropriate information. Because there is a lack of understanding about the importance of the interrelationship between institutional research and institutional planning, there is usually only limited information available at the different stages of planning and decision making. Too often, institutional researchers provide pages of data, but no necessary information. As a result, those responsible for planning are frequently unaware of the information that can be made available.

Since more and more pressure is being placed on postsecondary institutions to improve their planning, it is essential for institutional researchers to become more involved in supporting the planning process. The best way to create this involvement is to ensure that relevant and timely information is made available. Each of the chapters in this sourcebook attempts to show how institutional researchers can improve their ability to provide information that supports the planning needs of colleges and universities. If institutional researchers can develop and improve their reputation for providing necessary and timely information, then institutional research will flourish for many years to come.

N. P. Uhl (Ed.). *Using Research for Strategic Planning*. New Directions for
Institutional Research, no. 37. San Francisco: Jossey-Bass, March 1983.

References have been provided at the end of each chapter, but assessment of the external environment is such an important and formidable task that additional sources in two areas are presented here: Canadian research on the external environment, as well as other sources on futures research.

Canadian Sources Regarding the External Environment

As noted in Edward Sheffield's *Research on Postsecondary Education in Canada* (1982), the topics addressed by Canadian researchers are the same as topics addressed elsewhere, but Canadian research is more likely to be published as reports by the sponsoring organizations than in book form. Postsecondary education researchers in Canada can refer to the following sources for background on current issues of concern.

For Research on the Flow of Persons Through the System, Demographic Changes, and Enrollment Fluctuations

Picot, G. *The Changing Education Profile of Canadians, 1961 to 2000*. Ottawa: Statistics Canada, 1980.

Projects student age and educational attainment over the next twenty years, showing effects on the labor force and on the use of leisure time.

Science Council of Canada. *University Research in Jeopardy: The Threat of Declining Enrolment*. Ottawa: Science Council of Canada, 1979.

Examines consequences of the decline in participation rates in relation to the quality and effectiveness of university teaching and research.

Clark, W., Devereaux, M. S., and Zsigmond, Z. *The Class of 2001: The School-Age Population — Trends and Implications, 1961 to 2001*. Ottawa: Statistics Canada, 1979.

Stresses regional variations in the timing and degree of population fluctuations and enumerates other factors affecting postsecondary enrollment.

On Financing and Alternative Modes of Financing Postsecondary Education in Canada

Leslie, P. M. *AUCC Policy Study No. 3, Canadian Universities 1980 and Beyond: Enrolment, Structural Change, and Finance*. Ottawa: Association of Universities and Colleges of Canada, 1980.

A detailed analysis of financing alternatives for Canadian Universities and the probable impact of each alternative on the excellence of teaching and research. The study traces university development in Canada through the growth period of the 1960s to the uncertainty of the 1970s.

House of Commons. *Fiscal Federalism in Canada — Report of the Parliamentary Task Force on Federal-Provincial Fiscal Arrangements*. Ottawa: House of Commons, 1981.

Examines and recommends major programs under the Federal–Provincial Fiscal Arrangements, including the Established Programs Financing Act.

Economic Council of Canada. *Financing Confederation Today and Tomorrow: Summary and Conclusions.* Ottawa: Economic Council of Canada, 1982.
Analysis of federal–provincial fiscal arrangements.

Nowlan, D. M., and Bellaire, R. (Eds.). *Financing Canadian Universities: For Whom and by Whom?* Toronto: University of Toronto Institute for Policy Analysis, 1981.
Background for current discussion surrounding the renegotiation of federal–provincial fiscal arrangements and the Established Programs Financing Act.

On Work and Employment

Clark, W., and Zsigmond, Z. *Job Market Reality for Postsecondary Graduates.* Ottawa: Statistics Canada, 1981.
Labor market experience of the class of 1976, with a detailed analysis of survey results for sixty-two fields of study.

Devereaux, M. S., and Rechnitzer, E. *Higher Education — Hired?* Ottawa: Statistics Canada, 1980.
Exploratory overview of sex differences in employment characteristics of 1976 postsecondary graduates.

House of Commons. *Work for Tomorrow — Employment Opportunities for the '80s. Report of the Parliamentary Task Force on Employment Opportunities for the '80s.* Ottawa: House of Commons, 1981.
Examines and reports on shortages in skilled trades and higher-skill occupations in Canada, in view of the economic development requirements of the 1980s.

Employment and Immigration Canada. *Labour Market Development in the 1980s. Report of the Task Force.* Ottawa: Employment and Immigration Canada, 1981.
Analyzes the composition of the supply and demand components of the labor market. Reviews trends likely to affect Canadian labor markets in the 1980s and considers implications for the direction of federal government policies and programs affecting these markets.

General Overview

Sheffield, E. *Research on Postsecondary Education in Canada.* Ottawa: Social Sciences and Humanities Research Council of Canada, 1982.
A review for the Canadian Society for the Study of Higher Education and the Social Sciences and Humanities Research Council of Canada.

Harris, R. S. *A Bibliography of Higher Education in Canada, Supplement 1981.*
Toronto: University of Toronto Press, 1981.

Canadian Journal of Higher Education.
The Journal of the Canadian Society for the Study of Higher Education serves as a medium of communication among persons directly involved in higher education in Canada.

Sources on Futures Research

A few journals, periodic reports, and organizations are listed here.

Journals

Futures: The Journal of Forecasting and Planning.
Publishes scholarly articles by European and American futures researchers. Bimonthly; nineteen pages; $65 per year. IPC Press, 32 High Street, Guildford, Surrey Gu1 3EW, England.

Futurics.
As well as reviews and announcements, contains researched articles on alternatives for the future. Quarterly; sixty pages, $15 per year. *Futurics,* Science Museum of Minnesota, 30 East 10th Street, St. Paul, Minn. 55101.

The Futurist.
Magazine of the World Future Society; for general audiences. Articles touch on a wide variety of possibilities for the future. Bimonthly; fifty-six pages; $15 per year. The World Future Society, 4916 St. Elmo Avenue (Bethesda), Washington, D.C. 20014.

Periodic Reports

Center for Futures Research Newsletter.
Update of the center's activities. Bimonthly; two pages; free. Center for Futures Research, University of Southern California, Los Angeles, Calif. 90007.

Footnotes to the Future.
Summarizes significant trends, as reported in current periodicals. Reports on meetings, courses, books. Monthly; four pages; $15 per year. Futuremics, Inc., 2850 Connecticut Avenue N.W., Washington, D.C. 20008.

Future Abstracts
Abstracts of futures-related publications on five-by-eight–inch cards. Monthly; forty-eight abstracts per issue; $110 per year. Futuremics, Inc., 2850 Connecticut Avenue N.W., Washington, D.C. 20008.

Future Report.
Covers predictions, plans, patents, and other indicators of things to come. Monthly; six pages; $48 per year. Foundation for the Future, Box 2001, Newburyport, Mass. 01950.

Organizations

Center for Futures Research, Graduate School of Business Administration, University of Southern California, Los Angeles, Calif. 90007.
Conducts multidisciplinary policy analysis and forecasting studies in economic, business, technological, and social areas.

Center for Integrative Studies, University of Houston, Houston, Tex. 77004.
Studies and projects major consequences of ongoing global trends. Analyses available in publications and occasional conferences.

Center for the Study of Social Policy, Stanford Research Institute, Menlo Park, Calif. 94025.
For government and industry. Conducts policy and planning studies in the public interest.

Institute for the Future, 2740 Sand Hill Road, Menlo Park, Calif. 94025.
Forecasts and plans studies for public and private sectors.

Resources for the Future, Inc., 1755 Massachusetts Avenue N.W., Washington, D.C. 20036.
Conducts futures research for natural resources and the environment. Holds conferences and issues reports.

Science Policy Research Unit, University of Sussex, Mantell Building, Falmer, Brighton, Sussex BN1 9RF, England.
Conducts research into various aspects of the long-term forecasting of social change. Examines methodological as well as substantive issues.

The World Future Society, 4916 St. Elmo Avenue (Bethesda), Washington, D.C. 20014.
General organization for anyone interested in the study of the future. Has divisions and local chapters.

Norman P. Uhl is professor of education at Mount Saint Vincent University in Halifax, Nova Scotia. Previously, he was associate vice-chancellor for research, evaluation, and planning at North Carolina Central University and research psychologist with Educational Testing Service. He is coauthor of the Institutional Goals Inventory.

Anne Marie MacKinnon is executive assistant with the Association of Atlantic Universities.

Index